EXECUTIVE ORDERS

Before you start to read this book, take this moment to think about making a donation to punctum books, an independent non-profit press,

@ https://punctumbooks.com/support/

If you're reading the e-book, you can click on the image below to go directly to our donations site. Any amount, no matter the size, is appreciated and will help us to keep our ship of fools afloat. Contributions from dedicated readers will also help us to keep our commons open and to cultivate new work that can't find a welcoming port elsewhere. Our adventure is not possible without your support.

Vive la Open Access.

Fig. 1. Detail from Hieronymus Bosch, *Ship of Fools* (1490–1500)

EXECUTIVE ORDERS. Copyright © 2025 by the Organism for Poetic Research. This work carries a Creative Commons BY-NC-SA 4.0 International license, which means that you are free to copy and redistribute the material in any medium or format, and you may also remix, transform, and build upon the material, as long as you clearly attribute the work to the author (but not in a way that suggests the author or punctum books endorses you and your work), you do not use this work for commercial gain in any form whatsoever, and that for any remixing and transformation, you distribute your rebuild under the same license. http://creativecommons.org/licenses/by-nc-sa/4.0/

Published in 2025 by punctum books, Earth, Milky Way.
https://punctumbooks.com

ISBN-13: 978-1-68571-278-5 (print)
ISBN-13: 978-1-68571-279-2 (ePDF)

DOI: 10.53288/0519.1.00

LCCN: 2025939054
Library of Congress Cataloging Data is available from the Library of Congress

Editing: Vincent W.J. van Gerven Oei and SAJ
Book design: Hatim Eujayl
Cover design: Vincent W.J. van Gerven Oei
Cover illustration: Matthew Thurber

Opinions expressed in this volume are not attributable to or necessarily endorsed by the editors or individual persons affiliated with the Organism for Poetic Research. Nor does the appearance of a contributor's name in the "We, the undersigned" section of this book indicate endorsement of all statements contained herein.

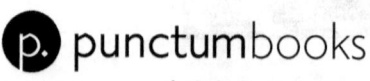

spontaneous acts of scholarly combustion

HIC SVNT MONSTRA

Organism for Poetic Research

EXECUTIVE ORDERS

Edited by Rachael Guynn Wilson
and Andrew Michael Gorin

Contents

Preface	11
Executive Orders	15
Postscript	183
Notes	189
Afterword	223
Bibliography	235
Acknowledgments	243

Preface

After the election of Donald Trump, a group of poets and activists conceived of a project wherein we could respond to the sudden and seemingly relentless barrage of Trump's dystopian executive orders with a series of our own. The project, titled "Executive Orders," was envisioned as a collaborative, freeform, "emergency" prose poem that would generate real-time responses to current events and the emerging American political landscape. The group began work on Google Docs, with the intention of drawing in new collaborators and publishing the text at various stages of its development. The result was a poetic catalog of the *people's* executive orders, orders that are at turns serious, absurd, satirical, philosophical, critical, utopian, and so on.

The first volume of *Executive Orders* was composed in January and February of 2017 and then published by The Organism for Poetic Research as a staple-bound zine in an edition of 50 copies. It had 15 contributors, was 43 pages long, and was distributed for free, with donations encouraged to activist organizations listed in the appendix. The second volume represented a continuation of the period of writing through March of 2018, and contained all that was in the first volume, plus substantive additions and revisions. It was the product of more than fifty contributors, some having participated in open writing sessions held in the lobby of the of the Brooklyn Public Library's central branch, and was published in collaboration with The Operating System. The third volume represented further continuation of the writing through February of 2020. It had over 100 contributors, many solicited at additional public writing events. It was published digitally by The Organism for Poetic Research for inclusion in Emily Carr University's online exhibition "Publishing the Present: An Archive of Mutual Care and Action." The fourth and final volume, which you are now reading, brings *Executive Orders* past the end of Trump's presidency and into its aftermath during the Biden Administration. This final and comprehensive iteration of the project has been revised and enlarged considerably relative to previous versions. While the bulk of the writing in *Executive Orders* was generated between 2017 and 2021, this volume also incorporates a coda with contributions gathered from late-2023 to early-2024 in anticipation of this publication. It also incorporates a new Afterword consisting of a conversation with the editors.

Executive Orders began as one literary community's efforts to cope with and respond to the tidal wave of reactionary policies enacted or proclaimed during the Trump years. As an index of historical happenings that follows events in rough chronological order (events including the Muslim-country travel ban, Black Lives Matter protests, the Kavanaugh hearings, the youth climate march, wildfires in Oregon and California, the January 6 riot at the Capitol, pro-Palestine protests and university encampments, and many more), it stands as a documentary record of this historical period from the perspective of mostly US-based artists, writers, leftists, progressives, and other participants whose identifications and political leanings we know not. It is also an experiment in crowdsourced collaborative making that tells a story about the ways we can — and *can't* — come together to form a virtual collective that may have a voice in political deliberations.

Executive Orders represents an exploration of the impacts and limitations of what philosopher J.L. Austin called "performative" utterances, speech acts that enact, or intend to enact, actual changes in the world. Inspired partly by Allen Ginsberg's famous poetic declaration of the end of the Vietnam War in his 1966 poem "Wichita Vortex Sutra," the project dramatizes the ambivalent fantasy and reality that inheres in such proclamations, at once undermining Trump's executive pronouncements while also holding out hope for the realization of our own. To this end, the text draws on relevant quotations that address, complicate, or even undermine its own grandiloquence and utopian aspirations — quotations from writers like Trinh T. Minh-ha, Jacques Derrida, and Claudia Rankine and Beth Loffreda. Further acknowledging that performative speech acts alone are not enough to create meaningful resistance and change, every version of *Executive Orders* has included an appendix that lists concrete actions one might take, and organizations one might support, in order to fight for social and environmental justice.

This project would not have been possible without the participation of the 89 named contributors and numerous anonymous contributors who are acknowledged as co-authors and signatories of the document in the "We, the Undersigned" section. Thank you for your orders. We will see that they take effect.

Rachael Guynn Wilson and Andrew Gorin, Editors
Brooklyn, 2024

Executive Orders

By the authority vested in us as the People by the Constitution and laws of the United States of America, we hereby order the ~~impeachment banishment~~ infinite rickrolling of the usurper Donald J. Trump

We decree henceforth an end to oligarchy, hierarchy, the patriarchy, and malarkey

We call for an immediate ban of plastic, cars, malls, big-box stores, and Facebook

We declare the immediate closure of the detention "camp" at Guantánamo Bay

Likewise for the Metropolitan Detention Center in Brooklyn, hole of darkness and assault, and the Metropolitan "Correctional" Center in Manhattan, reputedly worse than Guantánamo

We mandate that all National Parks employees use their Twitter accounts for POETRY ONLY!

We declare that science is poetry!

By the power of our bodies for our bodies, we acknowledge every citizen's right to health care, which shall be provided equally and to all

By the power drizzled over our persons by the Great Spaghetti Monster (who created the Earth with his noodly appendage), we order breadsticks

By the fleece vested in us, we order a freezer cake

By the vespers, we hereby declare an end to greed, manipulation, malice, the love of power and dominion

We believe that the abatement of these qualities in the population of the United States, and particularly in the rank(nes)s of its government, will serve the national interest

Accordingly, pursuant to our purslane, we shall eat salad

Let it be known that corporations are not, have never been, and never will be people

We unequivocally declare: domestic abuse is terrorism

Forced pregnancy is torture

Torture is capitalism

And capitalism is the reduction of life to the rule of syllogistic equivalency (i.e., exchange value)

As the United States is a nation predicated on theft, genocide, slavery, and systematic oppression, we order reparations for those who are historically and currently disenfranchised

The form reparations take shall be decided by those to whom they're due

We do not object to the complete reinvention of this society as the minimum threshold for reparations

We positively beg for it

Fig. 1. A tiled wall at the Union Square subway terminal in New York City is covered with sticky notes of various colors filled with notes and doodles by passersby. One group of notes near the center reads: "NOT MY PRESIDENT."

We declare that America is Mexico again!

We decree the taco trucks on every corner

That America is never one and always Turtle Island and Aztlán

That the separation of television and state be re-executed & reinforced

That the capitol shall be moved to the city of Flint, Michigan

Whatever Flint's drinking, our elected representatives are drinking

By the authority granted to our mouths by our larynxes, we hereby publish an end to all guns, bombs, drones, missiles, tanks, explosives, chemical weapons, gasses, pepper sprays, billy clubs, water cannons, grenades, mines, riot gear, cops, the military, bullies, shooters, terror, hate crimes, sieges, air strikes, battles, and war (declared or undeclared)

We declare an end to the military-industrial complex

"I lift my voice aloud,
 make Mantra of American language now,
  I here declare the end of the War!
   Ancient days' Illusion! —
    and pronounce words beginning my own millennium."

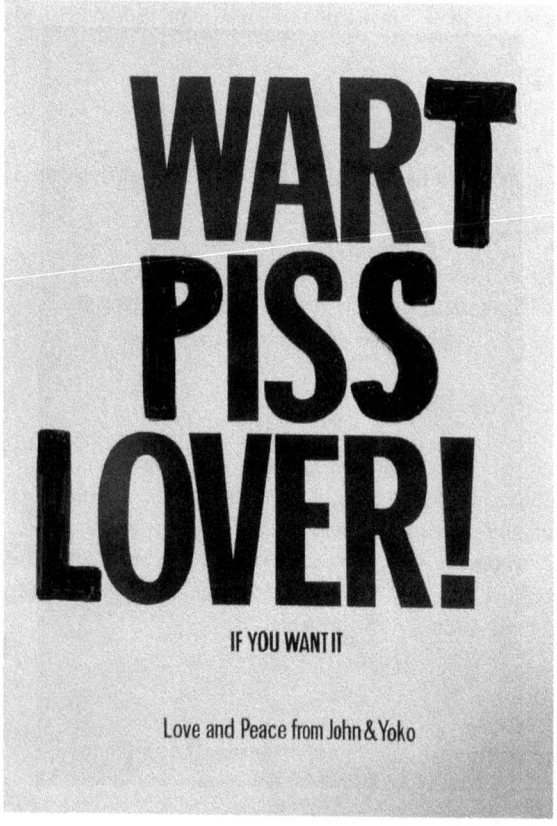

Fig. 2. Postcard image of John Lennon and Yoko Ono poster "WAR IS OVER! IF YOU WANT IT / Love and Peace from John & Yoko," altered to read, "WART PISS LOVER!"

The Department of Defense shall be reclassified as a research-only institution

Primary research goals of the new Department of Defense will include public health, climate change, and poetry

In an attempt to discourage the capitalist takeover of scientific thought, priority in funding will be given to basic science over applied science

In an attempt to counterbalance the long history of discriminatory practices against women in science, and the gender disparities that persist in scientific endeavors to this day, priority in funding will be given to grant applications submitted by principal investigators who identify as female

We declare all residents of the United States of America to be eligible for immediate and full citizenship

Fuck citizenship

We further issue an open invitation to all refugees, migrants, and immigrants. In particular, we invite the current citizens and residents of Iraq, Syria, Iran, Libya, Somalia, Yemen, and

Sudan to travel to the United States and remain here as long as they wish, enjoying the full rights of citizens

We additionally invite all the children of Iraq, Iran, Syria, Libya, Somalia, and Sudan to tea at the White House

The White House shall be transformed into a giant ball pit (the fun kind, as opposed to the giant ball pit it currently is)

By the power vested in us by the Earth itself, we declare the end of factory farming

Experiential learning courses in compassion and civic responsibility will immediately be implemented in all schools and workplaces

We demand that everyone just be cool for a second!

That, as permanent residents of the United States of America, we assume the right to vote in local, state, and federal elections

We further declare that "voter fraud" is a fraud

That deportation is kidnapping

That movement and migration are the inalienable rights of all living creatures

That these rights do not extend to colonizers and gentrifiers

Neither do they extend to corporations and currencies

That we shall not be evicted from our homes and dwellings

Let these homes and dwellings be defined both as structures and the complex sites that arise around them

That we dwell in Possibility (though some are forced to dwell in probability)

That Landlords shall return to their place among the Lobsterpeople

"Eia! for those who never invented anything
for those who never explored anything
for those who never conquered anything"

We decree a complete divestment from fossil fuels

2018 will be the first zero-carbon-emissions year in the history of the United States

All pipeline construction shall be terminated, effective immediately

Existing pipelines shall be dismantled and transported to Mar-a-Lago, where they will be repurposed as water slides for our new National Water Park

"Maybe the future USA should decide their presidency by having a soap-bubble contest"

Childcare shall be provided by the state at no cost to parents

Children shall be empowered to design their own school curriculum

Farmers, herbalists, plumbers, nutritionists, truck drivers, massage therapists, carry-out workers, and acupuncturists shall be well-compensated and respected

Mass public transit systems will be radically expanded

Highway systems will be subdivided and half the lanes will be fully separated and reserved for non-motorized vehicles

In all cities, bike lanes will be doubled in size, multiplied exponentially, and fully separated from car lanes and pedestrian areas

A series of well-maintained hiking trails will crisscross the United States

We announce that musicians, artists, and writers will be paid for their work!

Money is abolished!

Time is abolished!

Since the usurper Donald J. Trump built the mirrored walls along our Northern and Southern borders, Americans have become lost in a country reflected into an exceptional infinity. We declare an end to the American funhouse and order the demolition of the mirrored walls

…after one last nation-wide dance party!

"Let the States tremble,
  let the nation weep,
    let Congress legislate its own delight,
      let the President execute [her] own desire —
this Act done by my own voice,
      nameless Mystery —
published to my own senses,
  blissfully received by my own form
approved with pleasure by my sensations
  manifestation of my very thought
  accomplished in my own imagination
    all realms within my consciousness fulfilled"

By our electrical powers, we hereby decree an end to homelessness, shit jobs, depressing nursing homes, depressing hospitals, boring schools, crappy supermarkets, shitty food, and sweatshop labor

Furthermore, we order a ban on disposable bullshit, plastic bags, toxic crap, Muzak, tract homes, gated communities, the suburbs, SUVs, hunger and malnutrition, especially of the electrical soul

Everyone must say hello to four new people each week!

Everyone must come to the library!

By our prowess, let it be known that no one shall ever even think about questioning a woman's right to make decisions about her own body

Ditto a person's right to use the restroom of their own choosing

To protect our communities and better facilitate the gorgeous, borderless expanse, we mandate all buildings become wheelchair accessible. Less work culture, easier access to medication, more audio recordings, more ASL interpreters, more community healthcare, more resources to caregivers, more large print & braille

And that the basic economic unit will be that of care and nurturing, that no executive or worker will receive greater comfort or compensation in any form than those among us who wipe shit and drool, who clean, feed, clothe, and live in intimate service to the most vulnerable

We hereby declare:

Our sex-positive culture feels really good

More pleasure

Room for dessert

Anyone can walk down the street free of suggestion

What is a police state?

Banks are credit unions

Children are children

Actually, it *is* rocket science

Actually, there is, also, *science,* and we should pay attention

Climate change is real

Polar bears are vulnerable

Bees are a powerful resource

The people will be everyone, and everyone will be everybody

There will be infinite leisure for all

There will be spontaneous combustion

There will be spontaneous combustion of shitheads

There will be food, good health, long life, and joy for all

Mental illness bears no stigma

That we abolish the nation and nationalism

All borders are open for all time

We said: Borders will be open

Leave them in a better state than when you found them

Everyone is free

Everything is free

To acknowledge that we are guests on this land

That we roll out of bed from the never-ending, mediated waking and live our awareness

For a soft architecture made of un-noble materials

There will be a communal garden

Eat medicine from roots and trees

"So everyone is here"

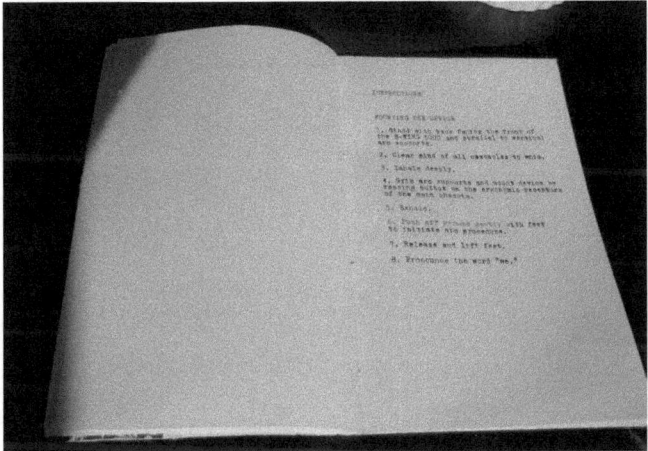

Fig. 3. A hand-sewn and typed pamphlet open to a page of "Instructions" that reads, "Mounting the Device: 1. Stand with back facing the front of the S-WING 5000 and parallel to the vertical arc supports. 2. Clear mind of all obstacles to whim. 3. Inhale deeply. 4. Grip arc supports and mount device by resting the buttocks on the ergonomic receptors of the main chassis. 5. Exhale. 6. Push off ground gently with the feet to initiate procedure. 7. Release and lift feet. 8. Pronounce the word 'we.'"

Reporting. There will be a blooming mushroom for President. Except as otherwise provided in this disorder, the Secretary and the Attorney General will consist of different kinds of mushrooms and each mushroom will seep and submit to the world a report on the spores of the directives contained in this disorder within 90 days of the date of this disorder and again within 180 days of the date of this disorder

Here's the ingredients list:
— Enriched corn meal (corn meal, ferrous sulfate, niacin, thiamine mononitrate, riboflavin, folic acid)
— Vegetable oil (corn, canola, and/or sunflower)
— Cheese seasoning (whey, cheddar cheese [milk, cheese cultures, salt, enzymes], canola oil, maltodextrin [made from corn], salt, whey protein concentrate, monosodium glutamate, natural and artificial flavors, lactic acid, citric acid, artificial color [yellow 6])
— Salt

Birdseed will not be forsaken. Crepey skin will move at the pace it wants to. Defects in the glass-making process will be given away as wabi-sabi charms. Big muscles will be used as paperweights and noses for sex in the dark

We demand:

For food to be spread around fairly

Summer (feeling) all year long

"Your hearts are
legislating Summer Weather now.
   Cancel Winter"

That all vehicles in the United States must run on renewable energy by ~~2030~~ 1988

Henceforth, all food and beverage establishments (restaurants, delis, etc.) across the country must compost and recycle ALL of their waste

"ANY CONGRESS MUST WORK ON THE PRINCIPLE OF THE
ARCHIMEDES SCREW
LOWER THE BIRTH AGE.
I SAID, 'LOWER THE BIRTH AGE'"

We decree the following national holidays:
— Frederick Douglass Day Where We Remember Who Frederick Douglass Is (February 1)
— Groundhog Day with Bill Murray Day (February 2)
— President's Day (April 1)
— Refugee Celebration and Support Day (April 15)
— Chinese Exclusion Act Day of Remembrance/National Day of Immigrant Appreciation (May 6)
— Juneteenth (June 19) [✓]
— Marsha P. Johnson Trans & Queer & Gender Non-Conforming Pride in Resistance Day (June 28)
— June Jordan Day of Poetry In the Streets (July 9)
— Howard Zinn Day (August 24; first day of the school year, to be spent in the study of American resistance movements)
— National Day of Mourning for Those Killed by National and International US Security Forces (September 11)
— Gloria Anzaldúa Day of Queer Love (September 29)
— Palestinian Liberation Day (November 15)
— Fred Hampton Memorial Day of Direct Action against White Supremacy (December 4)
— Day of Puerto Rican Liberation and Recognition (second Sunday in June)
— Interdependence Day (celebrated in space, not time)

We further decree:

Ignorance and vampirism are hereby abolished

The seas will be lemonade

All coastlines public

Dolphins will sing us to sleep

Organisms will dissolve and reconstitute at will

Purple rain

No more deaths

No more crying over me

The oceans will envelope us all and we will spontaneously produce gills

Your favorite stuffed animal will be Cactus-in-Chief

Though it's always been fucked, it will now be unfucked

Frederick Douglass is getting more and more recognized

Rosa Luxemburg is getting more and more recognized

Audre Lorde is getting more and more recognized

Frantz Fanon is an example of somebody who's done an amazing job

Emma Goldman is getting more and more recognized

Louise Bourgeois is getting more and more recognized

Aimé Césaire is getting more and more recognized

Theresa Hak Kyung Cha is an example of somebody who's done an amazing job

Judith Scott is getting more and more recognized

Romare Bearden is getting more and more recognized

Toussaint L'Ouverture is getting more and more recognized

Patrice Lumumba is an example of somebody who's done an amazing job

W.E.B. Du Bois is getting more and more recognized

Augusto Sandino is getting more and more recognized

Amiri Baraka is getting more and more recognized

Hildegard von Bingen is an example of somebody who's done an amazing job

Fig. 4. A poster titled "Insults Against a 1960s Environmentalist," 2022, by Amy Howden-Chapman, catalogs personal attacks made against environmentalist Rachel Carson.

By the plover nest in a tree, as Resident, by the Constipation and the loss of the Excited Stakes of Clamato, precluding the Conflagration and Fashionability Act (cfa) (33.3 E.S.C. 1090190310 et sex.), and in order to denture the rubric hefty of the Clamato people in communiqués across the Clamato Stakes, as well as to reassure the fallacy of the executive branch to be, we order, as follows:

The dankness

The perpetual reign of better ghosts

No forgetting

Gerrymandering is a cool new dance

The stars will continue to shine

All diamonds are put back in the earth

More singing

That landlords are a barbarism of the past

The state is officially withered

The answers to all the tests that are no longer happening because there will be no tests

Everyone an angel-headed hamster

Bowling Green will not be remembered

The lessons of the Greensboro Massacre will be known to all

"They talk to me about civilization, I talk about proletarianization and mystification"

No more lawns in the desert!

We have decided conflict minerals are not something we can live with

You can reach us on our landline

Children will worship dirt

They will be guided clearly from the inside

By the character of knowing, they will become the property of awareness

What is this globe?

A ball pocked with caves

so dark

that our eyes cannot penetrate the darkness?

We cannot bear to put our hands

through the waist deep shit

We will not touch our toes

Cannot stand the stench

Stand on the thorn

Whereas:

We live comfortably in our own haze

with just the remnant breeze of shit

which is only a reminder to wax poetic on suffering

Let it be known:

We request not to wax poetic on suffering

We demand to tear down prisons

We ask that all children speak from the glowing blue light of truth and clarity

Forever fighting against your lies and bullshit

My man won't let me garden

But I will grow food and build the soil

I will let my son eat the dirt we create. Maybe

I will shove it into every orifice of mine

In praise

I am wild

My ancients will be summoned

Compassion will entail, bloom, and spread

My ancients will be summoned

And will march and mutiny inhaling the gasses of humanity

Direct action through sneaking and knowing

Fig. 5. Sign affixed to a sapling growing in an NYC tree bed: "Please don't let your dog pee on our baby tree. Her name is 'Unless.'" Signed "Tahra Syo."

"Listen to the sound of the earth turning"

By the authority of good sense

And in opposition to the profane culture of convenience in America

The people have spontaneously and unanimously stopped using Solo cups

All citizens will compost their food waste and sort. their. recyclables!

"Our bodies are machines built to force so much
compassion and love and kindness into this world
that human life has no choice but to thrive and flourish"

We order that the oceans be saved

That humans learn to communicate with whales

That henceforward, all laws shall be made by blue whales

Until that time, the law shall be teal

shimmering

a rare duck

rustling

fragrant

an irregular solid

languorous

every other Tuesday

on special

lost between the cushions

meh

"Nevertheless, she persisted"

Section 1.
We decree that all life on earth has the inalienable right to clean air and water; this right is enforceable and shall be upheld by all individuals, states, and corporations

We mandate the creation of new habitat areas, wildlife protection areas, parks, greenways, and commons

Human-induced climate change shall be recognized as an imminent threat to life on Earth

We order that ICE be confined to its natural habitat: the North and South poles

We decree less car culture

Better scents in the city

More comfortable shoes

Lots of reading and lounging in parks

More picnicking, saunas in the woods, and refreshing swimming holes

More free, clean power generated by the sun

Everyone will be running into friends right when they are thinking of them

Social media is talking to your neighbor, the medium is the street

Section 2.
Definitions. As used herein and in Section 1 of this disorder, "inalienable" means *don't mess with us*

"Commons" shall have the definition set forth by sheep in their grazing

"Life" shall refer to the thing we're doing, viz. *chugging along,* and to all beings currently so doing

"ICE" has the meaning given to it by chemistry, namely, one atom of oxygen and two atoms of hydrogen bonded as a single molecule at a temperature at or below zero degrees centigrade or 32 degrees Fahrenheit

"Culture" has the meaning given to it by microbes

Except as otherwise noted, "scents" shall refer to subtle sensations in the nose

"Lounging" is defined as an act of resistance

"Friend" shall have the meaning given to it by another

"Street" has the meaning given to "commons" in Section 1 of this disorder, *baa*

Section 0.
"Can a writing that claims to break down rules and myths submit itself to the exclusive rules of a sociopolitical stand? Nothing could be more normative, more logical, and more authoritarian than, for example, the (politically) revolutionary poetry or prose that speaks of revolution in the form of commands or in the well-behaved, steeped-in-convention language of 'clarity'.... Writing thus reduced to a mere vehicle of thought may be *used* to orient toward a goal or to sustain an act, but it does not constitute an act in itself"

"If I say: 'I'm moving this chair,' I'm the one who is moving the chair and not the phrase that I emitted"

Section R
"The literary work and the political struggle will henceforth be undertaken simultaneously"

"Poetry will no longer give rhythm to action; it will be action"

Action, the film genre, will be devoted to acts of revolutionary empathy

Poetry, the film genre, will topple charts

"All the stores will open up if you / will say the magic words. The magic words are: Up against the wall mother / fucker this is a stick up!"

Section R&R
"…let's
turn off the power, turn on the
stars at night, put metal
back into the earth, or at least not take it out
anymore, make lots of guitars and flutes…
BLOW UP THE PETROLEUM LINES, make the cars
into flower pots or sculptures or live
in the bigger ones, why not?"

Chapter 33
By the pu-ehr tea in our cups, we declare that all stolen artworks and artifacts shall be repatriated

Corporations must disclose donations in public ads

Corporate banks are hereby abolished

Everything is cooperatively owned

For a federation of worker cooperatives to take the place of government

For the Great Mycelial Network to take the place of God

"Keep floating the idea of 'after America'"

Jerusalem is not the capital of Israel

I is not the capital of u

Capital is not the measure of a person's worth

Fig. 6. Handwritten sign posted on wall next to room number placard 302 reads: "Socialist Revolution Moved to 307."

We demand!

"que el hijo de puta franco no se ha muerto todavía"

That the usurper Donald J. Trump shall spend the remainder of his life in semi-exile, working for his sustenance, and meditating on the poor life he chose to lead

"son of a turd" after chrystos

That our anger remain the canary in this coal mine

Fly canary!

🐦 ☕ 🌱

♠ 🔥 ■

That "No one action will be adequate. All actions will be necessary"

From each, according to ability; to each, according to need

For now I must do the dishes

NO MORE PLASTIC
NO MORE PLASTIC
NO MORE PLASTIC
NO MORE PLASTIC
NO MORE PLASTIC
NO MORE PLASTIC

We decree that we are in no way pulling out of the Paris Climate Agreement

That the pullout method is NOT effective

That the Great Barrier Reef be saved

That oil tankers be repurposed as floating schools for anyone wishing to study sustainable aquaculture

By 2100 there will be more polar bears and more coral

Coal mines will be filled in, replanted, and rewilded

That all estuaries be refilled with oysters

All private pools are now public pools

Working railway infrastructure shall hereby be built, and it will be zippy and affordable

We shall chug pleasantly along the coasts and across the plains

We shall celebrate excellent broths

Section D
We're through with words used to D-grade people

We retain the right to the wor-D "shitbag"

We D-clare death to tyrants

We or-D-er the manufacture of more beautiful machines to kill fascists

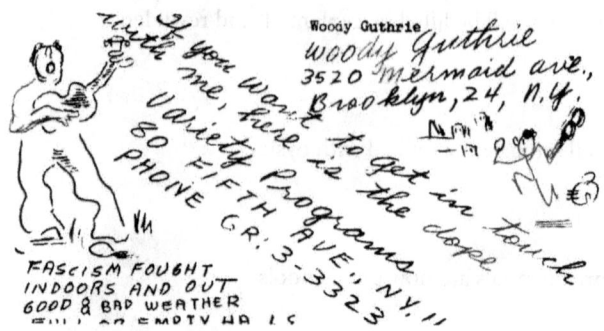

Fig. 7. Detail of a song booklet, "Ten Songs," by Woody Guthrie, with doodles and a handwritten note advertising a performance that reads: "Woody Guthrie, 3520 Mermaid Ave., Brooklyn, 24, N.Y. Fascism Fought Indoors and Out Good & Bad Weather."

We also decree:

No more famine

No despots

No baseless accusations

No shoes, no shirt, no servants

No tomorrow

No satellite radio

No cable TV

SECTION 8392.05 :: CARE/HEALTH/CARE/HEALTH/CARE
We hereby declare:

Healthcare that in fact includes both HEALTH and CARE shall be granted to ALL with no fear of repercussion

Sick days shall heretofore be referred to as CARE days and everyone can have an unlimited number of them. Folded into these are menstruation days and mental health days

Menstruation shall be celebrated and ritualized widely. Supplies shall be freely distributed in schools, ~~prisons~~ (there will be no prisons), workplaces, and other public spaces

Menopause shall be celebrated and ritualized widely. Hot flashes shall be honored with ice cream

By the compassion of two-million home care workers, we forthwith ratify: Healthcare is not a competition

I scream, you scream, we all scream for mental health services

Fig. 8. A 15th-century painting, *The Blessed Ranieri Delivering the Poor from a Prison in Florence,* by Stefano di Giovanni (Sassetta) depicts people fleeing a debtor's prison. Saint Ranieri gestures encouragingly to someone escaping prison through a hole in a wall.

Section Now:
The 13th Amendment shall be amended such that slavery will be fully, immediately, and unconditionally ended in the United States, with no exception for incarcerated persons

All of the prisoners will be freed and reparations shall be paid to all of the people who have been subjected to torture, including solitary confinement; to their families who have been harmed; and the descendants of any and all formerly enslaved individuals including formerly incarcerated people (our modern-day enslaved)

The United States of America shall no longer maintain a standing army

All those formerly employed by the military in the maintenance, support, and actions of a standing army shall be offered retraining as teachers, researchers, engineers, primary care physicians, clowns, allied health professionals, and poets

Meanwhile, all federal government funding that formerly went to the support and maintenance of the standing army shall be redirected to public school systems, public transit, and public health care

All FCC employees must be between the ages of 4 and 14!

Public access television shall be generously funded but will retain its low production values

The interstates laid out with minor literatures

Our relationships are freed forevermore from marketing data

We resolve that the facts of the former state of our lives, of our mistakes, be never be bought or sold, used as collateral, or begged from a distant administrator

That our paychecks be issued back to the 18th century in a timely manner

Roll back the clock: institute Climate-Savings Time!

That what we are primarily concerned with is being, not with what has been or may be lost

But that we are also concerned with what has happened, what was taken, and what is gone

That we search for what we have in common rather than focusing on what divides us

This in addition to appreciating and honoring difference

Embracing complexity, contradiction, conflict

As catalysts of transformative change

Like mist, it's mixed

For radical hearing happens when Tom Paine's "principles" and "right feeling" are supplanted by pink noise, flickering across the rooted-out fields of old torn flags

■→■== 🔥🔥🔥

And how do I explain my preference for a public body rather than any small-sized or tangible one simply trying to sleep?

And, if I ever fall asleep in a private body, who will I sleep beside?

And, if together we comprise a commune, how will I ever have the patience to read through the problems of living in it?

~~Stop knowing~~

Have faith that the universe is with me

Make everything a dollar or two cheaper

~~Equality~~ Equity is a human right

Create jobs for the disabled

Increase funding for art and education

Increase education in self-love

Art makes people happy

If you support happiness, support the arts

Fig. 9. Postcard of a Louise Bourgeois drawing, *Art Is a Guarantee of Sanity,* 2000, altered to read: "Art Is a Guanciale of Sanity," with a drawing of *guanciale* (cured pork jowls) added.

Punish big business, spread wealth

Eat better, hug, fuck, and shrug more

We shall all treat all people as people

Money is no longer considered speech

The citizens, united, hereby overturn Citizens United

We order that ~~half~~ 99.9% of the world be reserved for non-humans

We authorize birds to be bankers

We shall confront and reject any conception of freedom that requires or relies on the unfreedom of others

"EVERY HUMAN BEING IS AN ARTIST"

Witches are exonerated

You can steal a bed, but you can't steal sleep

It's all connected

Free Leonard Peltier!

We are all, have always been, and will ever remain in drag

If it doesn't bring joy, fuck it

Hitchhiking taught me to stand still

I declare, as one of a "we," or many "we"s: time, space, forms, and formats for knowing, sharing, and holding our lived and digital truths

We, as lichen-adjacent agents, declare the exclusive rights of lichen to define the collective, the individual, the planetary, the local, the symbiotic reality of more-than-human ecosystems, and express our collective desires for endless encounters, additions, and poetry

That it shall be the policy of the United States to protect the interests of brachiopods and indeed all pods, be they for small marine creatures or beans or TLC mp3s, all hail Lisa Left-Eye Lopez

We hereby order the immediate closure of all nuclear power plants and demand the systematic mapping and public disclosure of all existing nuclear waste. Copies of the aforementioned map to be distributed to every lawful (and previously unlawful) resident of the United States along with a complimentary glow stick

We declare the immediate phase out of all combustion engines, both for commercial and private vehicles beginning with, but not limited to, those vehicles frequently passing through "Asthma Alley" in the New York borough of the Bronx

We hereby re-invoke Executive Order 13653 of November 1, 2013 (Preparing the United States for the Impacts of Climate Change)

We hereby reverse the disbandment of The Interagency Working Group on Social Cost of Greenhouse Gases (IWG), and expand the powers of the working group to also consider the cultural cost of carbon

The Report of the Executive Office of the President of June 2013 (The President's Climate Action Plan) shall hereby be un-rescinded. The bureaucrats who, prior to the 2013 release of the report worked tirelessly to craft the document, are especially thanked for their committed and conscientious labour

NYC street sweeper machines will be replaced by brooms *swish swish*

Fig. 10. Photo of a patch of dirt, dead leaves, weeds, and trash strewn about by a Brooklyn apartment building, where a hand-painted sign reads: "<u>No</u> Garbage Here / No One — Ever!"

By Presidential decree, breastfeeding shall no longer be confined to small windowless rooms but shall be practiced and celebrated in public venues, including but not limited to parks, subways, street corners, cafes, and restaurants

We demand the immediate upgrading of all public transit stations with elevators and/or ramps to allow access by the disabled, and to those transporting infants, children, and heavy goods

We hereby order the reinstatement of all bans on the use of pesticides that the EPA's own scientists have proven are linked to the damage of children's nervous systems

Every child born on United States soil shall be gifted a bike and the inalienable right to ride it free from harm

Let the following declarations take to the land post-haste:

a) Gender and sexuality are not synonyms; henceforth they shall cease to be used interchangeably

b) Heterosexuality is not the default sexuality (yes, mother, I'm allowed to like girls)

c) Cisgender is not the default gender

a. All "gender reveal" parties are hereby canceled

b. Asking for a person's pronouns will be considered acceptable and shall no longer be done in hushed voices, but rather with pride and consideration

i. *Regardless* of proclaimed "grammatical correctness" (see statements made by the American Dialect Society along with common decency), the pronoun "they" shall be respected and used upon request

d) Binaries are hereby abolished

e) Attraction or lack thereof towards any human of any identification will no longer be considered a psychological disorder

    a. CONVERSION* THERAPY IS TO BE WIPED FROM THE FACE OF THE EARTH

f) Consent is mandatory when engaging in sex acts of any kind, regardless of the identities of the individuals partaking

g) Sexuality and gender shall be recognized as part of a larger scheme of social issues; they are not isolated topics

    a. Non-straight historic individuals shall be acknowledged as such in history courses across the nation in both primary and secondary schools

    b. The non-straight history of the United States shall be taught alongside similar civil rights movements

h) Pride merch will be free for anyone identifying as non-straight or for those who wish to support their children, step-children, parents, step-parents, grandparents, aunts, uncles, or black-sheep cousins

i) These declarations may be amended and added to so long as said amendments, addendums, or additions are rooted in open-mindedness, acceptance, and intersectionality. Amendments based in hate will not be tolerated

And finally:

No child, teen, or adult of any identification will need to fear the act of "coming out." No harm, physical or emotional, shall come to an individual who chooses to come out. In fact, all closet doors will be burned upon the request of their owner in a public and celebratory ceremony

*"No more conversion, no more conversation"

In addition, the following truths shall be acknowledged:

Climate change is real, Jesus Christ was brown, Christianity isn't the default religion, the prison system needs to be abolished, "homeless" and "drug addiction" aren't fucking synonyms, and so on and so forth

The "people who believe they are white" shall seek "a nobler basis for their myths"

And yet,

"I attest to this:

the world is not white;

it never was white,

cannot be white.

White is just a metaphor for power,

and that is simply a way of describing

Chase Manhattan Bank"

Fig. 11. Photo of Hans Haacke's *News, 1969/2008,* an RSS newsfeed printing a live news feed on continuous printer paper. A US flag hangs in the background.

You are hereby released from the scourge of busyness

"Know that in my heart I emailed you"

Productivity software will simulate serial staccato roars instead of neutralizing ambient noise

Cryogenic preservation will be regulated into oblivion and rich people will be forced to accept death

"'NOW THAT THIS IS THE NATURE OF REALITY THIS IS WHAT HAS TO HAPPEN:

(1) I NEED LOTS OF LOVE
(2) YOU'RE GOING TO GIVE US ALL YOUR MONEY 'CAUSE YOU HATE YOURSELVES AND 'CAUSE YOU KNOW
(3) ALL POWER SYSTEMS SELF-DESTRUCT WITH THE ADVENT OF ROBOT CANASTA PLAYERS WHO SHOW THE GIRLS WHAT THEY REALLY LIKE. I'M GOING TO SLEEP. GOODNIGHT.'"

All energy spent on self-flagellation is hereby redirected to rigorous dreaming

Famine is a moral failure with extra-moral consequences

The bodily starvation of the poor being a symptom of the spiritual starvation of the wealthy

We say fuck wealth and fuck hunger

Fuck rapacious consumerism and the cancers it vomits all over the world

Repent of capitalism and greed

No more war spectacle

Yes to rooftops

Yes to music

and multiple orgasms

Yes to seeing stars

We demand total harmonic freedom

We demand that the demands of the 1960s be made retroactive real

We demand full communism and until it has been achieved we demand excellent snacks

Alice Coltrane's "Journey in Satchidananda" is henceforth the US national anthem

We demand that you show fucking kindness to a sojourner

You yourself were a sojourner

Are

Sojourner

Sojourner

You are a sojourner

You filthy motherfucker

Fig. 12. Film still depicting a stone lion from Sergei Eisenstein's *Battleship Potemkin* (1925).

"By courageously looking, we defiantly declared: 'Not only will I stare. I want my look to change reality. Even in the worst circumstances of domination, the ability to manipulate one's gaze in the face of structures of domination that would contain it, opens up the possibility of agency. [… I]n all relations of power 'there is necessarily the possibility of resistance'"

weird weather day today. I've been watching it from bed all day as I'm trying to get over a very stubborn cold. the snow is sort of turning to ice on the branches out my window and at the same time flaking off in pillowy clumps like batting material. the sky is so blue it's hard to believe it was snowing this morning

talk soon!

"Paris will become a winter garden; fruit espaliers on the boulevard

"The Seine filtered and warm — abundance of precious stones artificially made — prodigality of gilding — illumination of houses — light will be accumulated, for there are bodies possessing this property, such as sugar, the flesh of certain mollusks, and the phosphorus of Bologna

"People will be ordered to paint the fronts of their houses with phosphoric substance, and its glow will light the streets

"Disappearance of evil with the disappearance of want

"Philosophy will be a religion

"Alliance of all nations

"Public festivals

"People will visit other earths — and when this globe is used up, Humanity will migrate to the stars"

Elon Musk will remain on Earth

Labor will no longer be subject to erasure

What are we, the proletariat, in both class and consciousness, to refuse ourselves?

The short answer is nothing

We shall make small steps in the infinite direction

Our hearts were not born with teeth but we learn to insert them

This signals the decline of an empire: millions of teeth in millions of hearts

What are we, the proletariat, in both class and consciousness, to do with ourselves?

We are to eat, shit, sleep, and never want again

"See, say, salvage.
Legislate.
Enact our inward law"

Make my puppy director of the Environmental Protection Agency

Make all heroes wear capes so you can know who to trust

It is legally required to flip any penny found facing tails to heads

All workers are required to wear a uniform hat unique to their respective trade

I am here to prescribe that every citizen of the United States of America wear a head covering constructed of aluminum foil with thickness of 0.016 mm and above. It is mandatory to wear such head cover between the hours of midnight and 9AM

"All the documentation will be published and mailed to each one of the collaborators to make a deep study of the language of the action, to the effects of calibrating its characteristics in a better and more effective incidence over reality"

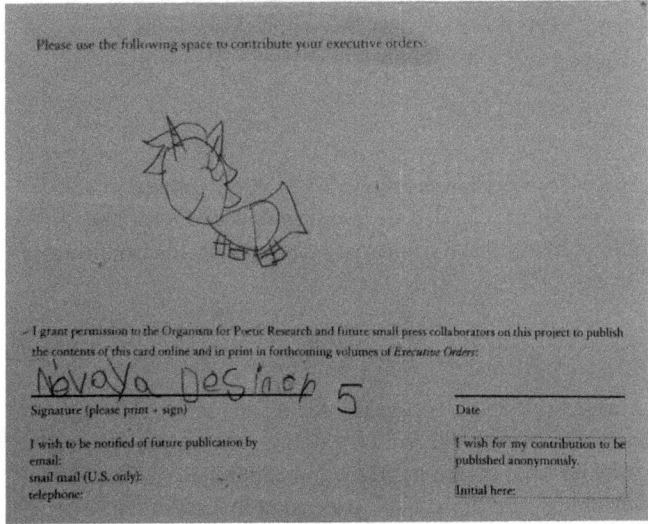

Fig. 13. Executive Orders submission card collected at a Brooklyn Public Library event held on September 21, 2019. The submission is a child's drawing of a unicorn, signed "Nevaya Desinor, 5."

Anyone can declare that they have the utmost anxiety about the problems that would occur if people were free from want and coercion. They can also declare that these future problems are worthwhile nonetheless

Anyone can declare that power is to be redistributed, if simply to reveal the character of those who would lose it and those who would stand to gain from its redistribution

Anyone can declare both a doubt and need of others, without shame. Anyone can declare this ambivalence is the beginning of honest relations and the end of fear

Anyone can declare that they do not know entirely what to do and anyone can declare that they do know what to do, although imperfectly. Both are cries for help, the beginning of attachment

Anyone may desire the pleasure and pain of others, but is not solely responsible for these desires. Our desires are not only ours, but shared in origin and continuance with others. Socialness is responsibility. The end of thoughtcrime and social amputations

Anyone can declare things are not simple, that existence is full of indifference. Anyone can declare we need not face such indifference in rivalry but in companionship. Anyone can declare this makes sense and yet pause. Anyone can be brave. Social life needs courage

Anyone can declare nature and nurture, without contradiction. It is good and bad to do what comes naturally and may be good or bad to go against it. Anyone can declare they are plastic

"This obscurity, this undecidability between, let's say, a performative structure and a constative structure, is *required* in order to produce the sought-after effect"

By the self-reflexivity of black holes, we declare:

Palm trees can pardon themselves

Flying squirrels can pardon themselves

Fountains can pardon themselves

Beluga whales can pardon themselves

Moods can pardon themselves

Giant clams can pardon themselves

Casement ledges can pardon themselves

Succulents can pardon themselves

Plateaus can pardon themselves

Mornings can pardon themselves

That monuments can and should fall

That monuments fall

That monuments are falling

By the power of ignorance, we hereby declare that the Governor of the US Virgin Islands is now the President of the United States of America

We declare no hesitation in declarations

We declare the B minor scale!

We declare knowledge and insight and love and care in and for all humans, aliens, life forces

We declare the end of the news cycle

We declare "fuck ton" as the new standard measure

We declare that our declarations will be the declamations of old women drinking tea by the fencepost

We declare angular and methodical and curved

We declare no gender

We declare that we have bodies that will not be wagered for the gain of the rich

We declare that the phrase "You're fired!" shall be replaced with the phrase "Congratulations, you've been liberated from the tedium of alienated labour!"

We declare the end of the false consciousness of violent fucks

We declare Black Lives Matter

We declare that gravity will end on Tuesday, November 6, 2018

We also declare that gravity will subtly change in strength and power to create acceleration until that date or such other date as we deem appropriate

We declare Love, Peace, Justice, with good vibration and comfort for most

By the powers vested in us by our bodies (those of us who have bodies, as well as those that do not, or have multiple, or who have simply visited a body for a while), we hereby declare:

That the skin is both illusion of border and border of river and mountain and of declarative words and gesture and intention so that all skin is sacred and beloved

That the Earth and the oceans and the sky and all flora and fauna are bodies and sacred and beloved too

That sleep will come to us all — a little sleep and a deep sleep — and we will glory in this world while we can

We declare that all Trans, Non Binary, & Gender Diverse / Variant ppls are hereby not only allowed, but encouraged, to live public lives: to consensually laugh, love, work, not work, eat, defecate, rest, dance, sing, recite poems, do cartwheels, wear clothing anticipating fashion futurisms for bodies not yet named, define or unravel themselves at will, whatever, whenever, amen, without threat to their autonomous bodies or communities from any imaginable form of violence. Period. Forever.

We declare that every day is right for power clashing your wardrobe

Everyone shall become a medievalist

No more mass shootings

No more "paralysis" on gun control

We declare the National Rifle Association (NRA) a terrorist organization

We declare that your heartbeat vibrates in my jaw bone like it is my own pulse, and we can rest in this moment of togetherness, a lucky cloud, and I am so grateful for your love

We declare Election Day a National Holiday. All employers are required to give employees a paid day off for the purposes of voting

All roofs shall be raised a minimum height of 30 inches

There will be a public bank

@realDonaldTrump does not exist!

Fig. 14. Person viewed from behind ascending NYC subway stairs with a piece of cloth pinned to their jacket that reads: "Donald Trump Is a Dangerous Parasitic Fascist."

That there shall be messiness & forgiveness

That there will be humanity

That we shall celebrate "the glorious tearing apart that life is"

That it will be a fight & a struggle

That usurpation is a constant & lifelong threat

Fig. 15. Audrey Wollen, a PSA brought to u by ur local chapter of Female Nothingness, October 2015.

"no gain is definitive"

We declare that no arts professionals can gain cultural capital from their rhetorical pronouncements of solidarity

We demand that all institutions looking for token artists of colour lose air conditioning in July and heat in January

We declare that curators should wear their compromises on their sleeves

"Consider this scenario, a caricature, I admit. An artist is contacted by a curator about a site-specific work. He or she is flown into town in order to engage the community targeted for collaboration by the institution. However, there is little time or money for much interaction with the community (which tends to be constructed as readymade for representation). Nevertheless, a project is designed, and an installation in the museum and/or a work in the community follows. Few of the principles of the ethnographic participant–observer are observed, let alone critiqued. And despite the best intentions of the artist, only limited engagement of the sited other is effected. Almost naturally the focus wanders from collaborative investigation to 'ethnographic self-fashioning,' in which the artist is not decentered so much as the other is fashioned in artistic guise. […] And this 'impossible place' has become a common occupation of artists, critics, and historians alike"

We decree:

Free and fair education

Free tampons! Free condoms! Free childcare!

Update our infrastructure

Apples are necessary

Apple is not necessary

Give more financial aid to grad students!

Lower taxes for the working middle class

Cancel all celebrities!

We, intersectional feminist sea monsters, globsters, and lobsters declare:

Neither the islands nor lowlands are sacrifice zones for waste and climate change

A 1.5-degree increase to be the benchmark for global warming

Reparations of money, love, and re-memory for already drowned low island spaces

New acid-resistant abodes for pteropods on the west coast of the untidy states, whose shells have dissolved

A refusal to accept the humanoid narratives of inevitable loss

So be it disordered

"Mon oraison, et toujours en français. Maintenant nous sommes toutes femmes. Les hommes sont morts. Tout le monde c'est femme et plus des femmes. Et parce que nous sommes femmes, nous sommes libres et fraîches. Adieu hommes. Merci déesse"

"This is the first time I gave my speech on the sidewalk. Now we are all women. The men are dead. There's just women and more women. Now that we are women, we are free and fresh! Goodbye men. Thank you, goddess"

By the power of the celestial sea, the Great Pacific and Atlantic Garbage Patches are hereby dissolved

In their stead, this loose conglomeration of bodies proclaims that we will no longer privilege the human and we will no longer privilege language as a means of communication

After a reasonable period of public review, the pathetic fallacy will be disarticulated into the sympathetic, antipathetic, parapathetic, surpathetic, and just plain pathetic fallacies

We will once again read the flights of birds, and we will no longer claim the Earth silent. Every city will establish a natural embassy, untouched by humanist planning and conservation

Effective immediately, no being is invasive

"Eeeeeenough about Human Rights, what about Whale Rights?

"What about Snail Rights?

"What about Bee Rights?

"What about Flea Rights?

"What about Ant Rights?

"What about Plant Rights?"

We hereby declare that

Anchovies are an endangered species

Consent is the best sexual orientation

We order the immediate and continuous disruption of the temporality of the endless update

The cynicism of planned obsolescence

Its wastefulness and negligence

We declare that people are not brands

People: you're not brands!

We declare the end of cryptocurrencies that run on lack of imagination, a surplus of ego, and an ecological deficit

We will fund research into cures for short-term amnesia

"Will the country become a gigantic supermarket, a floating casino, or a 'real' country? Will the new forms of thought vital to our survival ever emerge?"

There shall be foghorns in the night

"blu-a! blu-aa! Ao…"

After a period, everything's gently levitating

Everything, perched

Everything, winding and unwinding

And then, nothing

There is nothing

Nothing here for a long time

Monday, nothing

Tuesday, nothing

Wednesday, nothing

Thurdsay, nothing

Reading, nothing

Writing, nothing

Poetry, nothing

There was nothing here

This order intentionally left blank

What happened was, it'll wear you down

We carried signs that read: *This Is Not Normal*

Whatever that meant

So then

This comes into the inbox, from a collaborator's mother:

Executive Order of the first order: All sons will call their Mothers. At least once a week. Would it kill you? (March 27, 2018)

It was comforting, hearing from someone's mother like that

I was thinking: what would it be like to read this poem backwards?

Executive Order 13820 of January 3, 2018

Termination of Presidential Advisory Commission on **Election Integrity**

By the authority vested in me as President by the Constitution and the laws of the United States of America, it is hereby ordered as follows:

Section 1. Executive Order 13799 of May 11, 2017 (Establishment of Presidential Advisory Commission on Election Integrity), is hereby revoked, and the Presidential Advisory Commission on Election Integrity is accordingly terminated.

Sec. 2. General Provisions. (a) Nothing in this order **shall be** construed to impair or otherwise affect:

(i) the authority granted by law to an executive department, agency, or the head thereof; or

(ii) the functions of the Director of the Office of Management and Budget relating to budgetary, administrative, or legislative proposals.

(b) This order shall be **implemented** consistent with applicable law **&** subject to the availability of appropriations.

(c) This order is not intended to, and does not, create any right or benefit, substantive or procedural, **enforceable** at law or in equity by any party (other than by the United States) against the United States, its departments, agencies, or entities, its officers, employees, or agents, or any other person.

Then: Is this a poem?

I got sort of weary of the Executive Order as a form. Andrew and I were talking about it. When was the last time either of us had opened the Google doc

Had anyone else?

Amy cooked scallops and lemony risotto for the dinner party

That night it rained a proper New York City downpour and I was drenched in under ten seconds

The tragicomedy of it, trying to get into a car fast enough

The thing is, the news was relentless

I could swear it was giving me and everyone else I knew cancer

Lately it had been "the wall," the government shutdown for over a month, the Roger Stone indictment,

and before that: Christine Blasey Ford, Brett Kavanaugh, the "migrant caravan," a cascade of #MeToo

There were many things we missed

Mist descended on the 2018 calendar year

a haze of emotional exhaustion

and cognitive disintigration

through which, much later,

we retrospectively re-viewed:

Fig. 16. Aerial view of smoke and devastation in Santa Rosa, California, after wildfires in 2018.

And we declared:

The 14 students and 3 staff members murdered in the Parkland shooting shall not have lost their lives but instead shall have formed a multi-piece jazz ensemble whose collective playing melts guns into puddles

Additionally, children and young adults who have experienced a mass shooting shall never have had their deaths and near-death experiences counterfactually denied by pro-arms groups and individuals; they shall never have been called "crisis actors" or anything of the sort; they shall not have been subject to ridicule by conservative media personalities and outlets; nor to venomous personal attacks; nor shall they, their families, or the families of their murdered peers have received hate mail and death threats following the event

Additionally, no one shall have experienced multiple mass shootings

We order, retroactively, that we shall never have had to say any of this

We call B.S.
We call B.S.
We call B.S.
We call B.S.
We call B.S.
We call B.S.
We call B.S.
We call B.S.
We call B.S.
We call B.S.
We call B.S.
We call B.S.
We call B.S.
We call B.S.
We call B.S.
We call B.S.
We call B.S.

We also proclaim that children will not have been put in cages

That the migrant caravan shall have been received by a welcoming conga line of massage therapists

That Donald Trump and Kim Jong Un shall have been banished to a rocky outcropping on the Bikini atoll, where they are welcome to compare the size of their "nuclear buttons" (cancerous growths) all they want

All of Trump's properties shall have become the new homes of Syrian refugees displaced by violence incited by American "intervention"

Anti-cyberbullying initiatives shall be best modeled by Melania Trump's public denunciation of the Twitter account of her husband

People are not data

People: you're not data!

California is NOT burning

The Iran Nuclear deal is hereby official

There shall have been Zero Tolerance for the orange shit-stain-in-chief

Feb. 13, 2019
I still think about utopia

"Caw caw caw

crows shriek

in the white sun over grave stones in [Pittsburgh]"

Then, this part of the project becomes a diary

Figs. 17–20. From Sacha Archer's *Concrete Poems [Repurposed Executive Order]*, 2018, ink on paper.

The diary becomes collective

And since all diaries are about dreams

And dreams are yelps of the unconscious…

Or, since all diaries *are* dreams

And dreams are expressions of desire

And all desire is blue

Pale pale blue

Salmon and dusty yellow-brown

Electric purple and black

It becomes a painting

A drawing

A sculpture

A concrete poem

Feb. 15, 2019
Good things:

In response to public pressure, Amazon called off their corporate headquarters in Queens

Gray wolves have been taken off the endangered species list

Roma

The Squad

Fig. 21. Screenshot from Molly Crabapple's animated short "A Message from the Future with Alexandria Ocasio-Cortez, 2019."

Attribution studies

Black Lives Matter

Critical race theory

Anti-fascism

The kids

We demand the time of day

"At the tone, the time will be 12:32 a.m."

(you will dial 2 or 3. but please press 1
to register yr right to collectively
appear à tout suite)

We issue the following amendments to the articles of our speech:

AMENDMENT 1
a as in *aah* shall be used to express satisfaction
the shall refer to *the* ocean
an ocean shell see a sea anemone

AMENDMENT 1A
"Just because you have the right, doesn't mean that it's polite"

AMENDMENT 2
A well-regulated breakfast, being necessary to the prosperity of the gut microbiome, the right of bacteria to bear barms (*sic*), shall not be in fringe, or tassels

AMENDMENT 2.01

A well-defenestrated mistletoe, being unnecessary to the parity of the treetops, the light of the steeple as it peeks through the clouds, shall not be impinged

AMENDMENT −2

A well-negotiated mille-feuille, being necessary to the success of a dinner date, the delight of the plates to be cleaned or warmed, shell nuts shall be binged

Fig. 22. Franklin Furnace installation at Brooklyn Public Library main branch, September 2019. A banner hanging over one of the library's interior balconies reads: "Words Tend to Be Inadequate."

No more wrong notes

No more bullshit

No more wearing down of attention, just doing

No more toilet-dunking of cats

No more winning and losing

No more dying languages

Onay ormay yingday anguageslay

No more cow farts and no more cow-farting politicians

No more mass deportations and no more mass extinction

Fig. 23. Demonstrator holds a sign at the September 2019 climate march that depicts the Dr. Seuss character, the Lorax, flipping the bird. It reads: "The Lorax speaks for the trees and the trees say FUCK YOU."

We need more scavenger hunts

We need more dancing in the rain

A dog park on every block

Public bike shelters on every block (no more car parking privilege!)

Free dogs and doggie health care

Accessible mass transit!!

$100,000 from the government on your birthday (everyone's bday)

Free coffee all the time everywhere, anywhere, now…

Free fucking healthcare & free fucking haircuts & free fucking

City streets for pedestrians

Hay un mundo afuera de Nueva York

More tool libraries!

More music more music more music

For it is declared that Halloween is October…

The Mueller investigation is Halloween…

Russia is the president of the headless horseman…

Roger Stone is the Kremlin (and William Barr is a potato and cheese dumpling inside of a Matryoshka doll)…

Fig. 24. Stencil graffiti on a city sidewalk planter reads, "COMMUNISM IS STALINISM…." Below this, someone else has added in handwritten graffiti: "POP TARTS ARE DUMPLINGS."

The government shutdown
The government shutdown
The government shutdown
The government shutdown
The government shutdown
The government shutdown
The government shutdown
The government shutdown
The government shutdown
The government shutdown
The government shutdown
The government shutdown
The government shutdown
The government shutdown
The government shutdown
The government shutdown
The government shutdown
The government shutdown
The government shutdown
The government shutdown
The government shutdown
The government shutdown
The government shutdown
The government shutdown
The government shutdown
The government shutdown
The government shutdown
The government shutdown
The government shutdown
The government shutdown
The government shutdown
The government shutdown
The government shutdown
The government shutdown

End the longest ever government shutdown

Skolstrejk för klimatet!

There is no time to waste

Fig. 25. Extinction Rebellion information and signup table. Sign on the table reads: "Declare Climate Emergency."

Or,

We should waste all time in loving and leisure, not this exploitative overproduction and compulsory overconsumption

Brazilian Rainforest for President!

Jacinda Adern for head lemur!

House oversight for acting sea-turtle nest! (that the Hatch Act may be enforced)

Free the Rose Garden!

Free Hong Kong!

Free Ukraine!

Free Palestine!

Free Tibet!

Free snacks!

Everyone must inform themselves!

Only women are allowed to walk on the moon!

The Aliens, I want to know about the Aliens

Fig. 26. Copies of the Mueller Report titled, "Report on the Investigation into Russian Interference in the 2016 Presidential Election" by Special Counsel Robert S. Mueller, III, published in March 2019. A copy of the book lies open to a heavily redacted page.

O, Happy day! ... Whereas Nancy Pelosi, Speaker of the House, has announced that a formal impeachment investigation into the misdeeds of President Donald Duck shall commence,

Be it so ordered that Pez Dispenser Don Trumplione shall be swiftly and summarily impeached by the House *and* by the Senate

And that following his prompt removal from office, ordinary citizen Thump shall have his tax records delivered to the Manhattan District Attorney's office in response to their outstanding subpoena

And that if any wrongdoing is found, that citizen Thump shall submit to the maximum penalties for his crimes, including but not limited to the maximum prison sentence, to be served out in hours of community service, since prisons will be abolished; as well as monetary fines, which will be requisitioned and redistributed to the poor and working class in the form of practical tools, food, and choice knick knacks, since money will not be necessary in our post-capitalist society

And, should Mr. Trumpty gripe, crow, bluster, or threaten, that he shall receive a bigly itchy hairshirt, to be worn until sufficient remonstrance has been made

And that following the impeachment and removal of Mr. Clump from office, that this document shall be published in its entirety as *Executive Orders, Volume 3,* and the project shall conclude, with profound blessings and thanks, one volume sooner than anticipated

By the Autobahn viewed in utilities as the Percussion by the Contagion and the leeches of the Unmanly Statuaries of Amour, weasands hieroglyphically oust the immoderate impermeability of the utricle Donald J. Trump

By the custodial powers of the public and its library of active bystanders, we hereby proclaim:

No one-use plastic

No forest blues (fires)

That there shall be universal childcare leave for aunties & uncles, guncles & grandparents

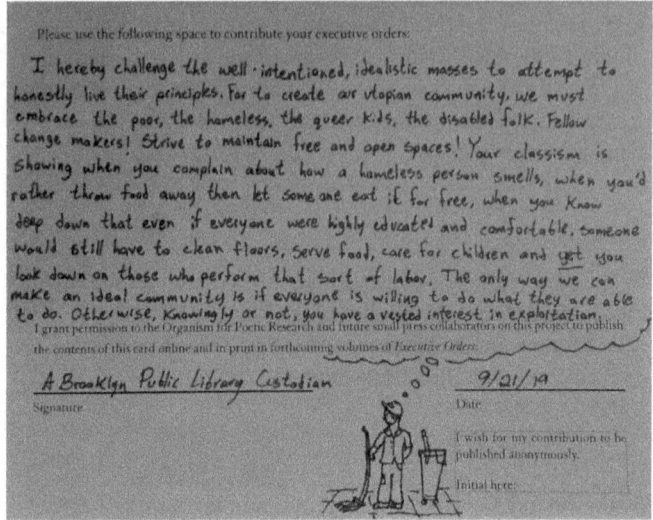

Fig. 27. Executive Orders submission card with cartoon of custodian with broom and garbage pail. The custodian's thought bubble reads: "I hereby challenge the well-intentioned, idealistic masses to attempt to honestly live their principles. For to create our utopian community, we must embrace the poor, the homeless, the queer kids, the disabled folk. Fellow change makers! Strive to maintain free and open spaces! Your classism is showing when you complain about how a homeless person smells, when you'd rather throw food away than let some eat it for free, when you know deep down that even if everyone were highly educated and comfortable, someone would still have to clean floors, serve food, care for children and yet you look down on those who perform that sort of labor. The only way we can make an ideal community is if everyone is willing to do what they are able to do. Otherwise, knowingly or not, you have a vested interest in exploitation." The card is signed: "A Brooklyn Public Library Custodian" on 9/21/19.

"Pour conjurer l'esprit de CATASTROPHE le chantage, la guerre des nerfs, du sexe, de l'œil et du ventre, la coercition du Père Noel Nucléaire, la terreur tricolore, la misère morale et son exploitation culturelle, la misère physique et son exploitation politique, l'Arte Moderne à genoux devant Wall Street (traverse de Liberty Street dans le bas Manhattan), la Commune de Paris oubliée au profit d'une École de crétinisation du même nom. Ca suffit comme ça. Il faut de librer à un exorcisme collectif"

"To banish the spirit of Catastrophe — blackmail, the war on the nerves, on the sexes, on the eyes and the stomach, the coercion of Nuclear Santa Claus, patriotic terror, moral misery and its cultural exploitation, physical misery and its political exploitation, modern art on its knees before Wall Street, the Paris Commune forgotten in favor of a stupid school of the same name. That's it. We need to perform a collective exorcism" It is hereby mandated, by the moral authority of the Anti-Hypocrisy League, that the central mission of every "prison education program" shall be prison abolition

All prisons shall be abolished

All police shall be abolished

Abolish the presidency

Abolish money

Neighbors shall lend each other eggs, give each other support, and help each other with the mundane

There shall be more trees and more parks

Add empathy and respect for your fellow humans

Closer communities

More libraries

Botanical gardens

More clean water faucets, drinking fountains, free public showers, and places where you can walk animals

I would like to change hatred into love

Let's smile at other smiling faces

Through the medium of the clear air

Let's remake our dreams, consider future generations, and create the systems for our planet to heal and regenerate

There will be social justice and equality

Everyone will be treated with dignity

We will tear down all cities and totally reimagine urban cultures

We will retrofit urban buildings and totally dig passive-heating-and-cooling architecture

We will imagine a place where a person is intrinsically motivated to unleash purpose into the work she brings to the world

More peace on Earth!

Stop littering

We will make the government and corporations work for us

We resolve "To fight the companies   to make somehow a future"

We will have joy in our lives

We will organize for radical change

i.e., revolution

An insistence endlessly enacted

Fig. 28. At a youth climate protest in New York in early spring 2019, elementary- and middle-school-aged persons stand behind a police barricade holding protest signs. In the foreground, a uniformed policeman has just thrown a large inflatable Earth balloon back into the crowd; it hangs in the air above the assembled protesters.

No justice, no peace

Fuck this racist police!

Hey, everybody, Donald Trump got impeached!!!

… oh… wait…

...

But that was just a dream we had

we slept and when we woke

the news was bad

er than we previously realized

damn

Or was it that we'd known all along???

"We seem to have new fire today,

in Napa county to the west, with ash falling

here and smoke obscuring the hills to the east,

My sister in Idaho lost much of her sheep ranch

to fire recently. The surviving ewes will spend the winter

elsewhere

as there is no barn, no feed. However the house

and garden escaped. As a result

they live in a sort of moonscape."

Wait a minute. Back it up.

The fires came on the heels of the protests

The protests came in the thick of COVID-19

COVID-19 came like a vulture

to hang in the air, indefatigable,

stalking the fetid, staggering nation

The virus attacked along well-worn lines

of race and class

Taking up our usual declamatory style, we decreed that all presidents — past, present, and future — were hereby infected with the novel coronavirus SARS-CoV-2

And that they be infected with antibiotic-resistant chlamydia (especially those that do not already have it)

At the same time, we did not wish disease or death on anybody

Instead, disease and death wished presidents on us

Here we are, every last resident, locked in our respective micro-neighborhoods

Socially distanced

And were we ever not socially distanced?

Would it feel half so bad, we wondered, if "we" were "in" this together?

As the saying goes: 同病相憐 ("common malady shared empathy")

Mid-May, the ambulance sirens were slowly replaced by the drone of police helicopters overhead

The cops corralled the protesters on the bridge, kettled the protesters still assembled at the moment the 8pm curfew went into effect in the Bronx

The police beat them ruthlessly — with batons, with bikes, rammed them with SUVs

Fired tear gas canisters and maced them

In Portland, in Kenosha, the police embraced as allies the white supremacist militias violently countering peaceful protestors, sometimes even murdering them

A nine-year-old girl states the case clearly, while officials look on in hand-wringing bemusement:

"I come here today to talk about how I feel. And I feel that we are treated differently than other people. And I don't like how we're treated just because of our color...We are Black people and we shouldn't have to feel like this. We shouldn't have to do this because y'all are treating us wrong. We do this because we need to have rights"

George Floyd

Breonna Taylor

Ahmaud Arbery

Rayshard Brooks

Jacob Blake

"I just saw a woman get her head bashed in because she walked away from an officer and didn't walk away fast enough. I saw a man exercise his constitutional right and say two words, and about 30 officers jumped on him. Did I wake up in another fucking country?"

8 minutes, 46 seconds later…

9 minutes, 29 seconds later…

"I believe *you* believe what happened," says the mayor, in response to a reporter's question. "We had observers for City Hall that saw a very different reality from what you saw"

"Last night in New York City, the NYPD was out there protecting us. Men and women of the NYPD. We ask so much of them. We ask so much strength, so much restraint"

"I have not seen the videos you refer to or seen those accounts. But if there's anything that needs to be reviewed, it will be"

"The NYPD has actually taken, I think, a very open approach respecting protest, flexible as always"

Oh, Feckless Mayor!

Were you ever more than a hot bag of stale subway air?

A handshake-and-smile-for-the-camera man?

A Saturday afternoon parade mayor, fit for a float?

A six-foot-five spineless wonder?

Oh, Mayor de Blah, there is nowhere left to be late for

There is nowhere left to forget in

Nothing to be late for — look at the time! Amy Coney Barrett has usurped the seat of the late SUPREME court justice, the Honorable Ruth Bader Ginsberg

Amy Coney Barrett ascends to the high court bench

"Boo! Boo! Boo! Bow to the Queen of Slime, the Queen of Filth, the Queen of Putrescence. Boooooo. Boo! Rubbish. Filth. Slime. Muck. Boo! Boo! Boo!"

We declare a new political party: the Break-Up Party

The Break-Up Party's single-issue platform calls for the immediate dissolution of the United States of Uh-uh 'merica

The platform is colloquially called Am-axe-it

U break it U say bye bye to it

Buzz buzz buzz

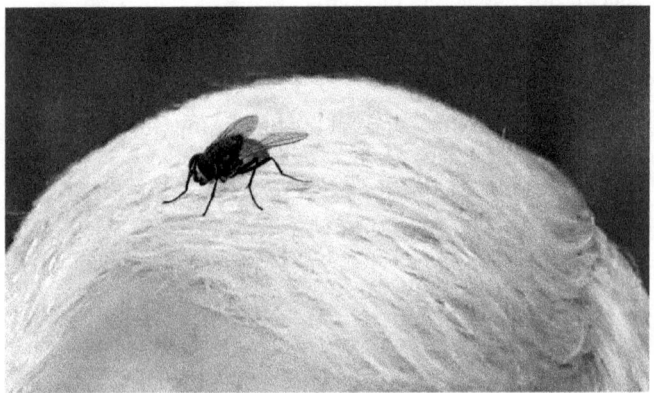

Fig. 29. A common housefly against the snowy white backdrop of Mike Pence's hair.

Oh, hello friend!

The fly injects its truth serum into the abominable snow-white scalp of Mike Pence

What's that you were saying, Vice President Pence?

"Just that my existence…

Fig. 30. The fly perches on Mike Pence. Closed captioning on the screen reads: "is a great insult to the men and women."

"Is a great insult to the men and women...

"of this country. You'd be enormous fools to believe me when I say...

Fig. 31. It's the 2020 Vice Presidential debate. The fly perches on. The closed captioning reads: "that President Trump and I stand with you."

"that President Trump and I stand with you.

"Of course we don't! That'd be like saying we care about the environment, healthcare...

Fig. 32. The fly remains affixed. The closed captioning reads: "and supporting our African-American neighbors —."

"and supporting our African-American neighbors —

"We don't even have African American neighbors! And if we did, we'd call the cops on them"

The truth serum wears off. The debate is over

We nominate the fly for the Medal of Honor and Nobel Peace Prize!

One month later…

na na na na

na na na na

hey hey hey

(Saturday, November 7th, 12 noon)

And C.A. Conrad swore to us on Zoom, September 22
(autumn equinox), that Georgia would go blue

The Heavens and Earth thank Stacey Abrams and all Georgia
activists, organizers, voters

The Washington Post may now change its slogan from
"Democracy Dies in Darkness" to "Democracy Flourishes
under the New Socialism"

Ok, ok… *The Washington Post* may now change its slogan from "Democracy Dies in Darkness" to "Democracy Withers in the Twilight"

Covid-19 on the rise

Fig. 33. Rudy Giuliani hosts a press conference about Trump's challenge to the 2020 election results at Four Seasons Total Landscaping in Holmesburg, PA on November 7, 2020.

November 7th: 240,000 deaths from Covid-19 in the U.S. alone

& no concession to Biden's victory

No concession to the will of the voters

No concession to "democracy"

Not even to their sacred cow, the electoral college!

They say "Stop the Steal" and it's a religion

They say "Stop the Steal" and it's a cult

They try to pressure Georgia to undo the vote

To "find" "11,000" "missing" Trump votes

They try to pressure Michigan to undo the vote

Pennsylvania, Arizona, Texas, Nevada, and Wisconsin

They try and try 'til Rudy Giuliani's black hair dye runs

In sweat-mixed rivulets down his temples

"Did you all watch *My Cousin Vinny?* You know the movie? It's one of my favorite law movies, because he comes from Brooklyn — And when the nice lady said she saw — And then he says to her, 'How many fingers do I, how many fingers do I got up?' And she says, 'Three.' Oh, she was too far away to see it was only two! These people [the poll observers] were further away than My Cousin Vinny was from the witness. They couldn't see a thing"

That's November 19, 2020 and 257,766 us dead from Covid-19

The machinery is breaking down

Convulsing madly

December 8th and 11th, the Supreme Court rejects two separate lawsuits seeking to overturn the election results

December 11, 2020 and 311,253 U.S. dead from Covid-19

Even William Barr can't go this far (December 14 resignation memo, effective December 23)

Is Melania as mad about Christmas this year as last?

"I'm working like a — my ass off at Christmas stuff… I say that I'm working on Christmas planning for the Christmas, and they said, 'Oh, what about the children? — that they were separated.' Give me a fucking break"

December 25th: 356,236 U.S. dead from COVID-19

Oh, Melania, "I really don't care — do u?"

Fig. 34. Melania Trump steps into a black SUV while on visit to migrant "detention" centers at the US–Mexico border in June 2018. She wears an army-green Zara jacket with the phrase "I REALLY DON'T CARE DO U?" emblazoned on the back.

Early January 2021, more than 60 lawsuits have failed to overturn the election results

January 6th, after demonstrators in the "Stop the Steal" rally breach the US Capitol building by force, eight Republican senators and 139 House representatives vote against certifying the election results in one or more states

Josh Hawley, R-Missouri

Ted Cruz, R-Texas

Tommy Tuberville, R-Alabama

Roger Marshall, R-Kansas

John Kennedy, R-Louisiana

Cindy Hyde-Smith, R-Mississippi

Cynthia Lummis, R-Wyoming

Rick Scott, R-Florida

January 6th and 387,253 U.S. dead from COVID-19

5 more dead at the Capitol

January 13, 2021, a second impeachment, and not a moment too soon!

Let's impeach all presidents!

(But Donald Trump twice)

Let the impeachment trial begin!

Setting: The Senate Floor, one month after the Capitol insurrection

Players:
Senator Mitchy "Mouse" McConnell
Senator Chucky "Cheese" Schumer
Rudy Giuliani as "My Cousin Vinnie"
Marjorie Taylor Greene
Nancy Pelosi
Donald Trump's Tax Returns
Horned Rioter
Podium Guy
Senator Lindsay Graham "Cracker"
Senator Bernie Sanders and His Vermont Mittens
His Vermont Mittens
Senator Ted "Shrimp Cocktail" Cruz
Confederate Flag
The Ghost of Rush Limbaugh

Act I, Scene I

Nancy Pelosi enters the Senate Chamber to deliver the article of impeachment from the House.

Nancy Pelosi: I'm Nancy Pelosi, the Speaker of the House, and I'm here to deliver the article of impeachment, and to distribute commemorative pens. Would anyone like a pen?

Senator Chucky "Cheese" Schumer: Thank you, Speaker Pelosi. I'll take a pen.

Nancy Pelosi: Anyone else? [*She walks among the senators handing out pens.*] While you're doodling during the trial, I want you to use this pen, and remember: they wanted to put a bullet in my noggin'!

Senator Mitchy "Mouse" McConnell: Thank you, Speaker Pelosi.

Freshman representative Marjorie Taylor Greene strides onto the Senate floor. She's wearing a red-white-and-blue-spangled jumpsuit and a charm bracelet laden with diminutive American flags and pewter Qs. Her Covid-19 mask bears the silkscreened image of Donald Trump's mouth, open mid-harangue. When she speaks, there's a sense of dislocation as MTG's voice emerges from Trump's mouth.

MTG: My fellow congressmen and women. O, great people of the Qunited States of Anonymerica!

Chucky "Cheese" Schumer: What's she doing here?

MTG: I stand before you today as an outsider to the Washington Swamp.

Mitchy "Mouse" McConnell: Let her speak, Chucky! She's new around here — you heard her.

MTG: Like Dorothy in the Land of Oz, I've traveled a long road to Capitol Hill, but it wasn't paved with golden bricks, I can assure you of that. It truly can be said: God only knows how I got here.

Horned Rioter: Amen, sister!

MTG: I am an outsider — to Washington, but also to so much more. Raised by nutria in the wilds of Milledgeville, Georgia, I'm hardly even human. This is why I can't be corrupted by the fetid Swamp air you breathe — and why I don't need this mask! [*Pulls mask off face.*] Pee-eww! does this trial stink to high heaven! I have it from my trusted Facebook sources that the so-called "insurrection" was started by George Soros, and you're all crisis actors! God save The DONNNNNALD!!!!

Mitchy "Mouse" McConnell: Ms. Greene, you're going to have to put your mask back on, or you'll be escorted out of the building.

MTG: I'll never go!!

Horned Rioter: I'll defend you! [*Horned Rioter rushes to her side.*]

Senator Lindsey Graham "Cracker": Mitchy, can we let her keep the mask off if she sits there quietly? She's been through enough as it is… Those masks are so itchy, Mitchy.

Senator Bernie Sanders and His Vermont Mittens: [*seated in folding chair with arms and legs crossed, wearing winter coat and His Vermont Mittens*] I don't find them itchy.

Lindsey Graham "Cracker": Well, they itch her. Don't they, Margie?

MTG: Ugharghughhhhh. [*She collapses into the arms of Horned Rioter.*]

Act I, Scene II

Mitchy "Mouse" McConnell: Let's call the Confederate Flag to the witness stand.

Lindsey Graham "Cracker": Are we doing witnesses?

Mitchy "Mouse" McConnell: Uh, I don't know, I just assumed so. I mean, there's a lawyer here.

Lindsey Graham "Cracker": Oh, well, what the hell. What do you say, Chucky?

Chucky "Cheese" Schumer: Oh sure, witnesses, sure thing. Do we have a witness stand?

Podium Guy: I've got a podium. [*Poses for camera with podium.*]

Chucky "Cheese" Schumer: Well, then, let's proceed.

Podium Guy hoists Confederate Flag over the podium. Rudy Giuliani as "My Cousin Vinny" approaches the witness.

"My Cousin Vinny": So, whaddya think you were doin' here on January da 6th?

Confederate Flag: Washington, D.C. has always been on my bucket list. 2021 seemed as good a time to go as any. I hitched a ride with some Proud Boys, and we listened to nu-metal all the way to the capitol.

"My Cousin Vinny": Could you describe "nu-metal" for the ladies and gentlemen of the jury?

Chucky "Cheese" Schumer: There's no jury, Mr. Vinny.

Confederate Flag: Sure, I mean, it's basically the sonic equivalent of an energy bar: chalky and gummy at the same time, very bland but also pungent, like it was left in the glove compartment of an overheated car... You wouldn't call it food exactly, but it sort of occupies the same conceptual category.

"My Cousin Vinny": And did you and your Proud Boy associates willingly listen to this nu-metal music?

Confederate Flag: Oh yes.

"My Cousin Vinny": Would you say you even *liked* it?

Confederate Flag: I don't have musical tastes per se. I'm simply a cipher for white aggression and race hatred. Sometimes I act like that's not the point and I'm just super interested in antebellum history, and then I listen to a bunch of fife and drum music, but really it's all the same to me.

"My Cousin Vinny": And how many fingers am I holding up?

Confederate Flag: Three?

"My Cousin Vinny": It's two! I only got two fingers up! Your Honor, I rest my case.

Chucky "Cheese" Schumer: I'm not a judge, Mr. Vinny.

From the skin below McConnell's neck, a turtle's head emerges. It looks out, revealing bloodshot eyes. Its blunt beak swivels. It hisses pestilentially. McConnell blinks as the turtle sinks back into the soft flesh. McConnell removes his glasses, wipes the lenses, and replaces them.

Mitchy "Mouse" McConnell: This whole trial is unconstitutional. I move to strike it from the record.

Chucky: I'm not sure that's proper procedure —

Lindsey Graham "Cracker" pulls a small figure from his pocket. It appears to be a doll made from pantyhose, cotton balls, brown yarn, and black felt. It might resemble Brett Kavanaugh. He holds it up to his ear, nods, and replaces the doll.

Lindsey Graham "Cracker": No, I have assurances from the best legal minds.

Act I, Scene III

Mitchy "Mouse" McConnell: Now it's time to hear from former president Donald J. Trump's counsel. Mr. Trump will be represented today by the Ghost of Rush Limbaugh. Mr. Limbaugh's Ghost, we are ready to hear your defense.

A noxious cloud of blustery white gas wearing the presidential medal of honor materializes at the podium.

Ghost of Rush Limbaugh: This January, hundreds of thousands of people — Americans who have gotten tired of being ignored and lied about and smeared as racists by these very Democrats in the media and the popular culture, Americans who have gotten fed up with having elections stolen from them by the Democrats, including the White House — these people went to Washington. They weren't protesters paid by George Soros, the Democrat Party. The overwhelming majority of these Americans were well-behaved and respectful. These are Republicans. They don't raise mayhem… Republicans do not join protest mobs. They do not loot, and they don't riot. To the grand disappointment of many people. But a tiny minority of these protesters, and undoubtedly including some antifa Democrat-sponsored instigators, did decide to go to the Capitol to protest. We're supposed to be horrified by the protesters. Meanwhile, four years ago, a coup was launched in the Oval Office of Barack Obama to overturn the election results of 2016 — and not a single word of concern about the potential damage to our Constitution. No, they were just in denial: "We didn't do it, I don't know what you're talking about, Trump's got to go, Trump's poison." So, yeah, there's a lot of irony out there, and there's a lot of people calling for the end of violence. There's a lot of conservatives, social media, who say that any violence or aggression at all is unacceptable regardless of the circumstances. Well, I for one am glad that Sam Adams, Thomas Paine, the actual Tea Party guys, the men at Lexington and Concord, didn't feel that way. Ok, so, let's get started on the phones. Today's excursion into broadcast excellence!

Chucky "Cheese" Schumer: Excuse me, Mr. Limbaugh's Ghost, are we on the air?

Ghost of Rush Limbaugh: Now that I'm dead, I'm always on the air, Chuck! And we have a caller. Who's on the line?

Senator Ted "Shrimp Cocktail" Cruz: Hi Rush. This is Ted "Shrimp Cocktail" Cruz calling in from Cancún. I'm down here enjoying a little surf and sun, all-you-can-eat jumbo shrimp, and bottomless margaritas, ha ha ha ha, with my lovely daughters and wife.

Ghost of Rush Limbaugh: Hi, Teddy, that's great. You've earned a vacation. Let me give you a tip, because now that I'm dead, I can see the future: You're gonna want to stay in Cancún awhile, because it's getting chilly in Texas. Brrrrrrrrrrrrr. So, what are you calling about today?

Ted "Shrimp Cocktail" Cruz: Thanks for the tip, Rush. I just wanted to tell the Democrats that we will never concede this stolen election. Donald Trump is our greatest president. If he stepped in dog poop, I would lick the shit off his shoes. He's that great.

Ghost of Rush Limbaugh: Wow, thanks, Ted. That's what we like to hear. Hopefully it won't come to that.

Ted "Shrimp Cocktail" Cruz: Yes, but if it did, I'd be ready.

Ghost of Rush Limbaugh: That's really great. I think we have time for another caller. Caller, go ahead.

Trump's Tax Returns: Hi, hello, this is Donald Trump's Tax Returns.

Ghost of Rush Limbaugh: Whoa, hey there, I think you might have the wrong number.

Trump's Tax Returns: Is this the hearing? I'm calling in to testify.

Ghost of Rush Limbaugh: This is the *Senate* hearing. I think you're meaning to call into the hearing in New York…

Trump's Tax Returns: Well, I just want to say we're innocent! I don't know why anyone wants to hear from me anyway. There's nothing to hear and nothing to see! I can assure you, we didn't pay a cent in taxes. Not a cent! We're in-NO-cent.

Ghost of Rush Limbaugh: Mmmm, right. That's right. Also, folks, you should know that presidents, uh, don't have to pay taxes. They can just pardon themselves. From taxes. So, there you have it. Thanks for calling in. Do we have time for one more caller?

Lindsey Graham "Cracker": [*whispering*] Hi, Rush.

Ghost of Rush Limbaugh: And who's on the line?

Lindsey Graham "Cracker": [*harsh whisper*] I'm calling from inside the room.

Ghost of Rush Limbaugh: Ok, ok, you're kinda creeping me out, whoever this is…

Bernie Sanders and H.V.M.: Your time is up — all of you! We're sick and tired of your radio show and this impeachment trial that's going nowhere. We have enormous health care and economic issues, climate issues, that we have got to deal with!

His Vermont Mittens detach from Senator Sanders and ascend into the air 30 feet or so. Their zigzag patterns begin to glow a bright yellow-white. The mittens clap together and thunder resounds. Lightning bolts shoot from their rounded tops, burning craters into the stage while senators crouch in fear.

His Vermont Mittens: We hereby convict Donald J. Trump of incitement to insurrection, obstruction of congress, abuse of power, abuse of women, abuse of language, incitement to stupidity, incitement to vulgarity, obstruction of reason, obstruction of truth, obstruction of mental and physical well-being for so many citizens of Planet Earth. In consequence, he shall be banned forevermore from holding office, public or private. He shall have no office or offices, nor a lobby, nor lounge, nor a den, nor living room, not a breakfast nook, no meetings over lunch or golfing — in fact, no golfing ever. He shall never again give speeches, nor any manner of public address. He shall be limited to addressing an uppermost limit of 3 individuals simultaneously. He shall never again recite the "snake poem" on penalty of becoming a snake. His likeness shall appear in no place — not on TV, not on t-shirts or tour buses, not on buttons, coffee mugs, nor in statuette form, even parodic. His name shall be removed from all public-facing spaces. He shall be renamed. His name is now Don'T.

His Vermont Mittens have spoken.

H.V.M. shake in the air, and a golden light rains down from them, bathing the stage in a warm glow. Senators and all watch reverently, except for Senator Sanders who occupies a folding chair with an air of cantankerous nonchalance.

Curtain.

Fig. 35. Senator Bernie Sanders photographed in a winter coat and mittens, sitting in a folding chair at Joe Biden's inauguration on January 20, 2021, held outdoors during the COVID-19 pandemic.

Ooooh, and he's gone but not forgotten / There's a stink he's left that's rotten / A familiar smell / That doesn't bode so well / Reminds us of the heap of trash / dirty cash foundation / of this nation…

We decree the state of permanent pessimism that never loses its sense of humor or affection

We pronounce the desire to make proclamations as robust as ever

"we do it for
the stars over the Bronx
that they may look on earth
and not be ashamed"

For "a time will come when […] we shall light a vast fire with banknotes, bills of exchange, wills, tax registers, rent contracts and IOUs, and everyone will throw his purse into the fire…"

In preparation, we order good reading, good music, good food and drink, good feeling and good conversation

Additionally: dancing, laughter, dozing, dreaming, scribbling, drawing, singing, humming along, stretching, sitting still, doing and undoing, holding…

Holding open…

At ready…

So be it (continually) disordered

```
h h h h          h   h              h h h h
 a a a        a a a a a a a a        a a a
  n n          n n n n n n n n n      n n
   n n n n n n n n n n n n n n n n n n n n n n n n
              g g g g g g g g g g g g g g g
              g g g g g g g g g g g g g g g
              i n i n i n i n i n i n i n i n
              t h t h      t h t h
              e r e        e r e
               !!!          !!!
```

(Hang in there!)

CODA

Fig. 36. Flag made by Columbia University students protesting the Israeli siege on Gaza, hanging at the encampment on Columbia University campus. The flag reads: "WHAT ARE WE FIGHTING FOR / FINANCIAL DIVESTMENT / ACADEMIC BOYCOTT / STOP THE DISPLACEMENT / NO POLICING ON CAMPUS / END THE SILENCE."

We declare the end of American support for Israel's occupation

We declare the end of apartheid
        the end of refugee camps
        the end of indiscriminate bombing and displacement
        the end of historical erasure
        the end of settler colonialism
        the end of ethnic cleansing
        the end of genocide

We refuse all paradigms in which people may be regarded as "collateral"

"We've seen Palestinian mothers who have to write the names of their children on their hands — because the chances of them being shelled to death, of their bodies turning into corpses are so high"

We say: Never Again Is Gaza

We say: Never Again for Anyone

We recognize the right to boycott

Hey, (University) Presidents:

"If you were honest about wanting to build community, you would be focusing on divestment, but you're not because you're full of shit

Board of Governors, you shouldn't be governing shit

The Board of Trustees shouldn't be entrusted with shit

The President shouldn't be presiding over shit…

The position that you hold shouldn't even exist…

Fuck your norms. Fuck your notions of decorum, with your glasses of water all sitting around the room… There is dignity for yourself and no one else"

The United States will stop abusing its veto power in UN Security Council resolutions critical of Israel

Palestine will be recognized as a full member nation in the United Nations

We declare the ~~two state~~ ~~one state~~ no state solution

tbh the state shld natural-

ly wither away of itself post-revolution

"Jean Genet said that a homeland is a stupid idea, except for those who still don't have one

"Goytisolo, the Spanish poet, answered him: 'And when they have a homeland?'

"Genet said: 'Let them throw it out the window.'"

We, the Undersigned:

Kimberly Adams
Kate Angus
Jason Balish
Charles Bernstein
Annie Bielski
Heather Booth
Jso Boslai
Saronik Bosu
Maria Bowler
Ethan Breitman
Elijah Brewer
Elena Callahan
Kwesi I. Camara
Isabel Sobral Campos
Joe Cogen
Matthew Corey
Daniel Dalgo
Celia Daniels
Samuel DiBella
Karen Dockery

Ian Dreiblatt
Zateany Duroc
ELAE (Lynne DeSilva-Johnson)
Gabrielle Fazevedo
Robyn Glenn
Juan Gonzalez
Andrew Gorin
Jeff Grunthaner
Maryam Gunja
G. H.
David B. Hobbs
Amy Howden-Chapman
Kerrilee Hunter
MC Hyland
Bethany Ides
Alex Juhasz
Jake Kennedy
Janet Klein
Zane Koss
Anna Kreienberg
Tiziana La Melia
Chime Lama
Derek Lee
Rachel Levitsky
Barbara Lewis
Lina (age 10)
Lola (age 9)
Lisa M.
Sandy Mandel
Paco Marquez
Joshua Mathews
Arthur Menezes Brum
John Melillo
Lisa Merchel
Carol Mirakove
Jared Murphy
Raina Murphy

S. Musa
Lauren Neefe
Betsy Newman
Heyrling Oropeza
Pakeezah
Nate Preus
Kimberly Quiogue Andrews
Rejaur Rahman
Ronald S.
Odaul S. G.
Archibald Sadynayskiy
Elizabeth Scott
Tasmi Dhoalgup Sherpa
Joyce Shiffrin
imogen xtian smith
Kaisa Solim-Holt
Anne-Britt Starli
Courtney Stephens
Theo Stewart-Stand
Errol Styles
Garth Swanson
Orchid Tierney, sea-monster
Doris Vila Licht
Morgan Võ
Candace Weber
Eric Weiskott
Marina Weiss
Weze
Lenise Whitley
Rachael Guynn Wilson
Sparrow
Yuleri
A Brooklyn Public Library Custodian
Anonymous
Anonymous Pangolin
Anonymous Alligator
Anonymous Anteater

Anonymous Armadillo
Anonymous Auroch
Anonymous Axolotl
Anonymous Badger
Anonymous Bat
Anonymous Beaver
Anonymous Buffalo
Anonymous Camel
Anonymous Capybara
Anonymous Chameleon
Anonymous Cheetah
Anonymous Chinchilla
Anonymous Chipmunk
Anonymous Chupacabra
Anonymous Cormorant
Anonymous Coyote
Anonymous Crow
Anonymous Dingo
Anonymous Dinosaur
Anonymous Dog
Anonymous Dolphin
Anonymous Dragon
Anonymous Duck
Anonymous Dumbo
Anonymous Octopus
Anonymous Elephant
Anonymous Ferret
Anonymous Fox
Anonymous Frog
Anonymous Giraffe
Anonymous Gopher
Anonymous Grizzly
Anonymous Hedgehog
Anonymous Hippo
Anonymous Hyena
Anonymous Jackal
Anonymous Ibex

Anonymous Ifrit
Anonymous Iguana
Anonymous Koala
Anonymous Kraken
Anonymous Lemur
Anonymous Leopard
Anonymous Liger
Anonymous Lion
Anonymous Llama
Anonymous Manatee
Anonymous Mink
Anonymous Monkey
Anonymous Narwhal
Anonymous Nyan Cat
Anonymous Orangutan
Anonymous Otter
Anonymous Panda
Anonymous Penguin
Anonymous Platypus
Anonymous Pumpkin
Anonymous Python
Anonymous Quagga
Anonymous Rabbit
Anonymous Raccoon
Anonymous Rhino
Anonymous Sheep
Anonymous Shrew
Anonymous Skunk
Anonymous Slow Loris
Anonymous Squirrel
Anonymous Tiger
Anonymous Turtle
Anonymous Unicorn
Anonymous Walrus
Anonymous Wolf
Anonymous Wolverine
Anonymous Wombat

Excerpts from:

Allen Ginsberg
Aimé Césaire
Yoko Ono
Claudia Rankine & Beth Loffreda
M. Wander Groin
Gwendolyn Brooks
Madeline Gins
Amy Howden-Chapman
Mark Baumer
Trinh T. Minh-ha
Victor Hugo
Arthur Rimbaud
Diane di Prima
Morgan Bassichis
El Violinista Del Amor
Chrystos
Jon Stewart
Joseph Beuys
Frank O'Hara
Ta-Nehisi Coates
James Baldwin
Kathy Acker
bell hooks
Gustave Flaubert
Clemente Padín
Jacques Derrida
Etel Adnan
Audrey Wollen
Hal Foster
Moondog
Muriel Rukeyser
X González
Alexandria Ocasio-Cortez
Greta Thunberg
Jean-Jacques Lebel

Susan Coolidge
Kyoo Lee
Zianna Oliphant, Charlotte, North Caroline
David Perez, Mott Haven resident
Bill de Blasio
The Ancient Booer (William Goodman)
Mike Pence
Rudy Giuliani
Melania Trump
Rush Limbaugh
Wilhelm Weitling
Amiri Baraka
Queen Rania of Jordan
Rutgers Student
Mahmoud Darwish

Postscript

Performative speech acts have an effect on the world. But alone they are not enough to create real resistance and positive change. Please consider taking the following actions as a means of realizing the orders executed above.

~~HELP IMPEACH THE USURPER DONALD TRUMP~~
~~Go to: https://impeachdonaldtrumpnow.org/~~

GET INVOLVED WITH A ~~2020 2022 2024~~ 2026 ELECTION
    CAMPAIGN
Find a local swing race at Swing Left: https://swingleft.org/
Go to Justice Democrats: https://justicedemocrats.com/
Go to Brand New Congress: https://brandnewcongress.org/
Fucking run for it: http://sheshouldrun.org/

FORM OR JOIN A LOCAL ACTION GROUP
Read: *Organizing for Social Change* by Bobo et. al.
See the Indivisible Guide: https://www.indivisibleguide.com/
Check out the Resistance Manual Wiki: https://www.resistancemanual.org/Resistance_Manual_Home
Organize a mutual aid network: https://www.mutualaidhub.org/

SUBSCRIBE TO AN ACTION EMAIL LIST OR NEWS SOURCE

Sign up for Daily Actions: https://dailyaction.org/

Sign up for the Weekly Action Checklist for Americans of Conscience: https://jenniferhofmann.com/

Check out: http://thesixtyfive.org/home (formerly the "We're His Problem Now" calling sheet)

Check out Trump Watch at *Entropy*: http://trumpwatch.entropymag.org/

Update and view the People's Calendar: https://www.risestronger.org/events

CALL (OR SEND A POSTCARD TO) YOUR ELECTED REPRESENTATIVES

Find contact and other info for your representatives here: http://act.commoncause.org/site/PageServer?pagename=sunlight_advocacy_list_page

Or use Resistbot: https://resistbot.io/

READ, WATCH, AND SHARE WHAT YOU KNOW

Check out Trump Syllabus 2.0 at Public Books: http://www.publicbooks.org/trump-syllabus-2-0/

Check out "A Time for Treason" at *The New Inquiry*: http://thenewinquiry.com/features/a-time-for-treason/

Check out this Standing Rock syllabus: https://nycstandswithstandingrock.wordpress.com/standingrocksyllabus/

Read this Black Lives Matter syllabus: http://www.blacklivesmattersyllabus.com/fall2016/

Read and reread the M4BL platform: https://policy.m4bl.org/

More resources here: http://www.theoperatingsystem.org/citizenresources/

FOLLOW, DONATE TO, VOLUNTEER FOR, OR GET INVOLVED WITH THESE ORGANIZATIONS

350.org

ABC No Rio

Al Haq

American Civil Liberties Union (ACLU)
American-Arab Anti-Discrimination Committee
Americans for Immigrant Justice
Amnesty International
Anarchist Black Cross
Anera
A.N.S.W.E.R. Coalition
Bash Back
Big Brothers Big Sisters
Black Lives Matter
Border Angels
Boycott from Within
Brand New Congress
BYP100
Campaign Zero
Center for Reproductive Rights
Citizenship Through English
Climate Science Legal Defense Fund
Communist Party USA
Cooperative Economics Alliance of NYC
Council on American-Islamic Relations
Democratic Congressional Campaign Committee
Democratic Senatorial Campaign Committee
Democratic Socialists of America
Desis Rise Up and Moving (DRUM)
Dignity for Palestinians
Disability Rights Education and Defense Fund
Doctors Without Borders
Emily's List
Environmental Defense Fund
Everytown for Gun Safety
Extinction Rebellion
Faculty for Justice in Palestine
Fight for Fifteen
Girls Write Now
GLAAD
HEAL Palestine

Human Rights Campaign
Humanity and Inclusion
Immigrant Defense Project
Immigration Impact
Interfaith Alliance
International Medical Corps
International Refugee Assistance Project
International Rescue Committee
International Socialist Organization
Jewish Voice for Peace
Jews for Racial and Economic Justice
Justice Democrats
Know Your IX
Make the Road New York
Metropolitan Anarchist Coordinating Council
Mexican American Legal Defense and Education Fund
NAACP Legal Defense Fund
NARAL Pro-Choice America
National Center for Transgender Equality
National Council of La Raza
National Domestic Workers Alliance
National Immigration Law Center
National Lawyers Guild
National Urban League
National Women's Liberation
Native American Rights Fund
Natural Resources Defence Council
New York City Antifa
New York Taxi Workers Alliance
The Octavia Project
Opportunities for a Better Tomorrow
Our Revolution
Oxfam International
Pacifica Network
Palestine Children's Relief Fund
Palestinian Academic and Cultural Boycott of Israel
Palestinian Youth Movement

Party for Socialism and Liberation
People for the American Way
Physicians for Human Rights
Planned Parenthood
ProPublica
Rape, Abuse & Incest National Network
Red Canary Song
Sacred Stone Legal Defense Fund
Safe Horizon
Sanctuary for Families
Save the Children
She Should Run
Showing Up For Racial Justice (SURJ)
Sierra Club
Southern Poverty Law Center
Stand with Standing Rock
Standing Together
Students for Justice in Palestine
Sylvia Rivera Law Project
The Committee to Protect Journalists
The New Sanctuary Coalition
The Trevor Project
The United Nations High Commissioner for Refugees
The White Helmets
Transgender Law Center
We The Protesters
Young Artists Language and Devotion Alliance (YALDA)
Young Center for Immigrant Children's Rights

CONSIDER BOYCOTTING

Check out the #grabyourwallet boycott list: https://grabyourwallet.org/

Download the BoycottTrump app: https://itunes.apple.com/us/app/boycotttrump/id1171663655?mt=8

Check out Boycott, Divestment and Sanctions (BDS): https://bdsmovement.net/

MORE THINGS TO DO!

EXECUTIVE ORDERS

Divest from unethical corporations and fossil fuels!
Form a co-op!
Join a labor union!
Support grassroots media!
Do civil disobedience!
Go to protests!
Strike!
Make Art!
Make Community!

Notes

The following provides citations for quoted materials and elaborates on allusions to select historical events that occurred during the period of writing.

*We mandate … * POETRY ONLY!   In January of 2017, the Trump administration temporarily suspended the social media privileges of the Department of the Interior after the National Parks Service published images showing Trump's inauguration crowd side-by-side with Barack Obama's in 2009. The administration additionally placed gag orders on the Environmental Protection Agency and Department of Agriculture. In response, rogue Twitter accounts associated with the National Parks Service began tweeting about climate change and in opposition of President Trump, who had called climate change a hoax.

Fig. 1   This crowd-sourced installation was organized by Matthew "Levee" Chavez for "Subway Therapy," a project Levee initiated before the 2016 election, but which ballooned in the aftermath. The notes were eventually removed by the Metropolitan Transit Authority (MTA) in cooperation with Chavez on Dec. 16, 2016. Photo by Alba Vigaray/EPA.

We decree ... every corner Marco Gutierrez, co-founder of Latinos for Trump, stated in an MSNBC interview on September 1, 2016, "My culture is a very dominant culture, and it's imposing and it's causing problems. If you don't do something about it, you're going to have taco trucks on every corner." See Adrian Florido, "Picture an America with #TacoTrucksOnEveryCorner," *NPR,* September 2, 2016, https://www.npr.org/sections/codeswitch/2016/09/02/492446419/picture-an-america-with-tacotrucksoneverycorner.

That the ... Flint, Michigan The predominantly African American city of Flint, Michigan began having problems with its water supply in April of 2014 after it started drawing water from the Flint River. In 2015, it was found that Flint's water contained dangerously high levels of lead. In January of 2016, Rick Snyder, the Republican governor of Michigan who had served since 2011, declared a state of emergency. It's estimated that nearly 30,000 children were exposed in Flint to high levels of lead, which is known to cause major long-term health and cognitive problems.

We further ... and Sudan Trump issued Executive Order 13769, Protecting the Nation from Foreign Terrorist Entry into the United States on January 27, 2017. The order banned travel to the United States from seven Muslim-majority countries, temporarily suspended refugee resettlement, and lowered the refugee admissions quota for the fiscal year. This order was blocked in the court case of *Washington vs. Trump* on February 3. However, Trump subsequently issued several related executive orders and presidential proclamations.

"I lift ... own millennium" Allen Ginsberg, "Wichita Vortex Sutra," in *Planet News: 1961–1967* (City Lights, 2001), 119.

Fig. 2 *Wart Piss Lover (if you want it),* 2023, altered postcard by Rachael Guynn Wilson.

"Eia! for ... conquered anything" Aimé Césaire, *Notebook of a Return to the Native Land* (Wesleyan University Press, 2001), 36.

"Maybe the ... soap-bubble contest" Yoko Ono, *Grapefruit: A Book of Instructions and Drawings by Yoko Ono* (Simon & Schuster, 1964), n.p.

Trump built ... Southern borders Trump issued Executive Order 13767, Border Security and Immigration Enforcement Improvements on January 25, 2017. The order called for "the immediate construction of a physical wall on the southern border."

"Let the ... consciousness fulfilled" Ginsberg, "Wichita Vortex Sutra," 119.

By our ... own body Trump issued a Presidential Memorandum Regarding the Mexico City Policy on January 23, 2017, thereby reinstating a Reagan-era ban on granting federal funding to international organizations that offer abortion counselling or advocate for abortion rights. This was the first of Trump's official acts curtailing abortion access.

Ditto a ... own choosing The Trump administration issued a Dear Colleague Letter, revoking Obama-era guidelines protecting the rights of transgender students to use bathrooms that reflect their gender identities, on February 22, 2017.

"So everyone is here" Claudia Rankine and Beth Loffreda, "On Whiteness and The Racial Imaginary," *Literary Hub,* April 9, 2015, https://lithub.com/on-whiteness-and-the-racial-imaginary/.

Fig. 3 Detail of *S-WING 5000 Instruction Manual,* 2009, hand-sewn, stamped, ink-drawn, and typewritten pamphlet, edition of 1, by M. Wander Groin. This instruction manual was written as a guide to using the S-Wing 5000, which was discovered in an attic in Iowa City, Iowa, and installed on a porch there the same year the manual was created.

"Your hearts ... Cancel Winter" Gwendolyn Brooks, "BOYS. BLACK. *a preachment,*" in *Beckonings* (Broadside Press, 1975), 15.

"ANY CONGRESS ... BIRTH AGE" Madeline Gins, *What the President Will Say and Do!* (Station Hill Press, 1984), 31.

Frederick Douglass ... more recognized Trump remarked on February 1, 2017 that "Frederick Douglass is an example of somebody who's done an amazing job and is being recognized more and more, I notice." He was speaking at an event with African American supporters on the first day of Black History Month. Reporters noted that Trump's remark — both its nonspecificity and its present tense construction — seemed to indicate that he did not know who Frederick Douglass was. See, for example, David A. Graham, "Donald Trump's Favorite Topic for Black History Month: Himself," *The Atlantic,* February 1, 2017, https://www.theatlantic.com/politics/archive/2017/02/frederick-douglass-trump/515292/.

Fig. 4 Amy Howden-Chapman, *Insults Against a 1960s Environmentalist,* 2022, screen printed poster, 21 × 29.5 inches, edition of 50. The poster presents a catalog of personal attacks made against writer and environmentalist Rachel Carson after her critical exposé of the chemical industry, *Silent Spring* (Houghton Mifflin, 1962).

Bowling Green ... to all On February 2, 2017, advisor to President Trump Kellyanne Conway referred to a "Bowling Green Massacre," supposedly carried out by Iraqi refugees. This event never occurred.

The lessons ... to all On November 3, 1979, in Greensboro, North Carolina, members of the Ku Klux Klan and the American Nazi Party fired upon demonstrators in an antiracist march organized by the Communist Workers Party. Five demonstrators were murdered and eleven injured.

"They talk ... and mystification" Aimé Césaire, *Discourse on Colonialism*, trans. Joan Pinkham (Monthly Review Press, 2001), 43.

"Listen to ... earth turning" Ono, *Grapefruit*, n.p.

"Our bodies ... and flourish" Mark Baumer, "Our Bodies Are Machines Built to Force so Much Compassion, Kindness, and Love into the World Human Life Has No Choice but to Thrive and Flourish," *Barefoot Across America*, November 10, 2016, https://notgoingtomakeit.com/my-body-is-a-machine-built-to-force-so-much-compassion-kindness-and-love-into-the-world-human-a5d492d874e5. Baumer recited a variation on this phrase, which is also a poem, on November 9, 2016, day 28 of his barefoot walk across America and the day after Donald Trump was elected president. See Mark Baumer, "A guy who doesn't believe in human induced climate change gave me a dollar," *YouTube*, November 10, 2016, https://www.youtube.com/watch?v=CdV2AlU88UY.

"Nevertheless, she persisted" This phrase was first used by Senate Majority Leader Mitch McConnell to disparage the behavior of Senator Elizabeth Warren at the confirmation hearing of Jeff Sessions as Attorney General of the United States on February 7, 2017. The phrase was quickly adopted as a feminist slogan. Warren had criticized Sessions's record on civil rights.

We order ... South poles Trump signed Executive Order 13768, Enhancing Public Safety in the Interior of the United States on January 25, 2017. This order stated that "sanctuary jurisdictions" such as sanctuary cities would no longer be eligible for federal grants unless they complied with federal immigration enforcement measures, including those carried out by Immigration and Customs Enforcement (ICE).

"Can a ... in itself" Trinh T. Minh-Ha, *Woman, Native, Other: Writing Postcoloniality and Feminism* (Indiana University Press, 1989), 16.

"The literary ... undertaken simultaneously" Graham Robb, *Victor Hugo: A Biography* (W.W. Norton & Company, 1997), 178–79.

"Poetry will ... be action" Arthur Rimbaud, "Letter to Paul Demeny," May 15, 1871. Translated from the French by unknown translator.

"All the ... stick up!" Amiri [LeRoi Jones] Baraka, *Black Magic: Poetry 1961–1967* (Bobbs-Merrill, 1969), 225.

"... let's turn ... why not?" Diane di Prima, *Revolutionary Letters* (City Lights Books, 1971), 46.

"Keep floating ... 'after America'" Morgan Bassichis, *The Odd Years* (Wendy's Subway, 2020), 39.

Jerusalem is ... of Israel Trump signed a Presidential Proclamation Recognizing Jerusalem as the Capital of the State of Israel and Relocating the United States Embassy to Israel to Jerusalem on December 6, 2017.

"Que el ... muerto todavía" El violinista del amor & los pibes que se miraban, *Contra Los Fantasmas: Canciones e Himnos de Revoluciones Que No Fueron* (Buenos Aires, 2013), digital album, https://elviolinistadelamorylospibesquemiraban.bandcamp.com/album/contra-los-fantasmas-2013.

"son of a turd" Chrystos, "They Always Tell Me I'm Too Angry," in *Fugitive Colors* (Cleveland State University Poetry Center, 1995), 45.

NOTES TO PAGES 52–66

"No one ... be necessary"   Jon Stewart, qtd. in Marissa Martinelli, "Jon Stewart Turns a Late Show Bit About Trump's Executive Orders into a Rousing Call to Action," *Slate*, February 1, 2017, https://slate.com/culture/2017/02/jon-stewart-reads-fake-trump-executive-orders-to-stephen-colbert-on-the-late-show-video.html.

We decree ... Climate Agreement   Trump announced on June 1, 2017 that the United States would withdraw from participation in the 2015 Paris Agreement on climate change.

Fig. 7   Woody Guthrie, "'Ten Songs' booklet, with holograph additions, 1945." From the Collection: *Hughes, Langston, 1902–1967.* Beinecke Library. Box: 443, Folder: 10402. Call Number: JWJ MSS 26, Series XI. https://archives.yale.edu/repositories/11/archival_objects/346317.

Fig. 8   Stefano di Giovanni [Sassetta], *The Blessed Ranieri Delivering the Poor from a Prison in Florence*, 1437–1444, tempera and gold on poplar panel, 43 × 63 cm, Musée du Louvre, Paris.

The 13th ... incarcerated persons   The 13th Amendment to the United States Constitution provides that "Neither slavery nor involuntary servitude, except as a punishment for crime whereof the party shall have been duly convicted, shall exist within the United States, or any place subject to their jurisdiction."

Radical hearing ... "right feeling"   Thomas Paine (b. 1737, England) was a political writer, abolitionist, and American and French revolutionary remembered most for his *Rights of Man* (1791) and *The Age of Reason* (1794).

Fig. 9   *Art is A Guanciale of Sanity,* 2023, altered postcard by Rachael Guynn Wilson.

The citizens ... Citizens United   On January 21, 2010, the US Supreme Court sided with the conservative nonprofit group

Citizens United in a 5–4 majority ruling in *Citizens United v. Federal Election Commission.* According to The Brennen Center for Justice, the decision "reversed century-old campaign finance restrictions and enabled corporations and other outside groups to spend unlimited funds on elections." As a result of the ruling, "corporations can now spend unlimited funds on campaign advertising if they are not formally 'coordinating' with a candidate or political party." *Citizens United v. FEC* led to the growth of super PACs (Political Action Committees without spending limits) and "dark money" (defined as "election-related spending where the source is secret"). See Tim Lau, "Citizens United Explained," *Brennan Center for Justice,* December 12, 2019, https://www.brennancenter.org/our-work/research-reports/citizens-united-explained.

"EVERY HUMAN ... AN ARTIST" Joseph Beuys, qtd. in Willoughby Sharp, "An Interview with Joseph Beuys," *Artforum,* December 1, 1969, https://www.artforum.com/features/an-interview-with-joseph-beuys-210674/.

We are ... in drag On March 2, 2023 Tennessee Governor Bill Lee signed Senate Bill 0003, banning drag performances from occurring on any public property in the state, as well as in any location where minors could be present. Tennessee became the first state in the country to criminalize drag performances. Later in 2023, Texas and Montana passed their own anti-drag laws, while states such as Florida and Alabama attempted to pass similar laws only to have them legally blocked or dropped due to public protest.

"All the ... over reality" Clemente Padín, *Toward a Language of Action,* c. 1976, Offset announcement, Gronk Papers, UCLA Chicano Studies Research Center.

"We declare ... the Bronx" Mott Haven is a neighborhood in the South Bronx that is sometimes called "Asthma Alley" because of its air pollution levels. Residents of Mott Haven "need asthma

hospitalizations at five times the national average and at rates 21 times higher than other NYC neighborhoods." Researchers and journalists have pointed to Mott Haven as an exemplar of "environmental inequality." See Hazar Kilani, "'Asthma Alley': Why Minorities Bear Burden of Pollution Inequity Caused by White People," *The Guardian*, April 4, 2019, https://www.theguardian.com/us-news/2019/apr/04/new-york-south-bronx-minorities-pollution-inequity.

We hereby ... Climate Change Executive Order 13653, Preparing the United States for the Impacts of Climate Change, was signed by President Barack Obama on November 1, 2013. This presidential order set out broad areas in which to direct federal attention and resources in preparation for the effects of climate change. On March 28, 2017, President Donald Trump issued Executive Order 13783, Promoting Energy Independence and Economic Growth, which rescinded Executive Order 13653. (This was where things stood at the time of the writing in this volume to which this note refers.) Four years later, on January 20, 2021, President Joe Biden issued Executive Order 13990, Protecting Public Health and the Environment and Restoring Science to Tackle the Climate Crisis, which revoked or suspended a slew of anti-environmentalist executive orders issued by Trump, including Executive Order 13783, thereby effectively reinstating Executive Order 13653.

We hereby ... of carbon The Interagency Working Group (IWG) was created in 2009 by President Barack Obama to quantify "the net harm to society" of adding one ton of emissions of greenhouse gases a year, and "to create consistent estimates for use across agencies" drawing on "the best available science." President Trump disbanded the IWG in March 2017 and President Biden reinstated the IWG in January 2021. See "The Social Cost of Greenhouse Gases (Carbon Dioxide, Methane, Nitrous Oxide)," *Environmental and Energy Law Program, Harvard Law School*, https://eelp.law.harvard.edu/tracker/the-social-cost-of-carbon/.

EXECUTIVE ORDERS

The Report … conscientious labour The President's Climate Action Plan was an environmental plan to reduce carbon emissions that was first introduced by President Barack Obama in 2008 and subsequently updated every two years until 2013. President Donald Trump eliminated the Climate Action Plan on March 28, 2017, with Executive Order 13783, Promoting Energy Independence and Economic Growth.

We hereby … nervous systems On December 4, 2020, the Trump Administration "[r]ejected a proposed ban on chlorpyrifos, a pesticide linked to developmental disabilities in children." Additionally, "[i]n 2020, the E.P.A. also rejected its own earlier finding that the pesticide can cause serious health problems, though it later recommended some label changes and usage restrictions." Nadja Popovich, Livia Albeck-Ripka, and Kendra Pierre-Louis, "The Trump Administration Rolled Back More Than 100 Environmental Rules. Here's the Full List," *The New York Times,* October 16, 2020, https://www.nytimes.com/interactive/2020/climate/trump-environment-rollbacks-list.html.

i. Regardless … upon request On January 3, 2020, The American Dialect Society recognized the singular "they" first as their 2015 "Word of the Year" and again in 2020 as their "Word of the Decade." See "2019 Word of the Year Is '(My) Pronouns,' Word of the Decade Is Singular 'They,'" *American Dialect Society,* January 4, 2020, https://americandialect.org/2019-word-of-the-year-is-my-pronouns-word-of-the-decade-is-singular-they/.

"No more … more conversation" Frank O'Hara, *The Collected Poems of Frank O'Hara* (University of California Press, 1995), 475.

The "people … their myths"' Ta-Nehisi Coates, *Between the World and Me* (Random House, 2015), 7.

"I attest ... Manhattan Bank" James Baldwin, "Black English: a Dishonest argument," qtd. in Raoul Peck, dir., *I Am Not Your Negro* (Artémis Productions, 2017).

Fig. 11 Hans Haacke, *News*, 1969/2008. RSS newsfeed, paper, and printer. Dimensions and choice of news source variable. Installation photo at *Hans Haacke: All Connected*, New Museum, New York, 2019.

"'NOW THAT ... SLEEP. GOODNIGHT'" Kathy Acker, *Blood and Guts in High School* (Grove Press, 1989), 122.

"By courageously ... of resistance" bell hooks, *Black Looks: Race and Representation* (South End Press, 1992), 116.

Fig. 12 In *Battleship Potemkin* (1926), Soviet director Sergei Eisenstein explored and developed some of his most radical filmic montage techniques. The "lion sequence" is a frequently cited example of the rhetorical power of montage in film. Here, three shots of three separate lion statues (one sleeping, one lying down but awake, and another poised between sitting and standing) are sequenced to give the effect of a slumbering lion awakening and "rising up." Eisenstein splices this montage into the film at the conclusion of the fourth part, as the Potemkin's crew responds to the Cossack's civilian massacre by firing at the Odessa Opera House, where the Czar's generals are headquartered.

Eisenstein thought of montage as an aesthetic analog to the social contradiction that, per dialectical materialist philosophy, would lead to revolution. "[M]ontage is conflict," he writes, and: "Conflict lies at the basis of every art"; *"There is no art without conflict.* No art as process" (emphasis in the original). In Eisenstein's view, it was the "social mission" of art and artists to "reveal the contradictions of being." In so doing, the artist functions as agitator, spurring on political insurrection and provoking transformative societal changes. Sergei Eisenstein, *Selected*

Works: Vol. I, Writings, 1922–34, ed. and trans. by Richard Taylor (University of Indiana Press, 1988).

"Paris will ... the stars" Gustave Flaubert, *Bouvard and Pécuchet*, trans. T.W. Earp and G.W. Stonier (New Directions, 1954), 345–46.

"If I ... I emitted" Clemente Padín, *Toward a Language of Action*, c. 1976, Offset announcement, Gronk Papers, UCLA Chicano Studies Research Center.

"See, say ... inward law" hooks, *Black Looks*, 15.

"Know that ... emailed you" John Melillo, email to Rachael Guynn Wilson of April 28, 2021. This phrase was reported to be a meme, but the source could not be located.

"This obscurity ... sought-after effect" Jacques Derrida, "Declarations of Independence," *New Political Science* 7, no. 1 (1986): 9.

Palm trees ... pardon themselves Trump began exploring the possibility of pardoning himself as early as July, 2017. He subsequently asserted that he has the right to do so in tweets and comments.

By the ... of America On October 13, 2017, after returning to the US from a tour of locations hit hard by Hurricane Maria, Trump addressed a group of religious conservatives at the "Values Voter Summit," reporting that he had "met with the president of the Virgin Islands." Trump appeared to be referring to Governor Kenneth Mapp and to have forgotten or not understood that the President of the Virgin Islands was himself. Josh Delk, "Trump Refers to Virgin Islands Governor as Its 'President,'" *The Hill*, October 13, 2017, https://thehill.com/blogs/blog-briefing-room/355377-trump-calls-governor-of-virgin-islands-its-president/.

We declare ... Lives Matter The Black Lives Matter movement originated in 2013 when activists circulated the hashtag #BlackLivesMatter on social media after the acquittal of George Zimmerman in the killing of Trayvon Martin. The movement continued to grow up until and in response to events that occurred during Trump's presidency, including the murder of George Floyd by police officer Derek Chauvin in 2020.

We declare ... November 6, 2018 November 6, 2018 was the date of the midterm elections that occurred two years into Trump's presidency. As a result of these elections, Democrats gained control of the House of Representatives, ending Republican control of both chambers of Congress.

That we ... life is" Etel Adnan, *Of Cities & Women: Letters to Fawwaz* (Post-Apollo Press, 1993), 45.

Fig. 15 Audrey Wollen, a PSA brought to u by ur local chapter of Female Nothingness, digital image, October 2015.

"no gain is definitive" Adnan, *Of Cities & Women*, 37.

"Consider this ... historians alike" Hal Foster, "The Artist as Ethnographer," in *The Traffic in Culture: Refiguring Art and Anthropology,* eds. George E. Marcus and Fred R. Myers (University of California Press, 1995), 306–7.

A 1.5 ... global warming Under the 2015 Paris Agreement on climate change, signatory countries agreed to work to limit average global temperature to under 1.5 degrees of warming. On October 8, 2018, the Intergovernmental Panel on Climate Change (IPCC) published a Special Report on Global Warming of 1.5°C.

"Mon oraison ... Thank you, goddess" Sparrow, impromptu speech (first given in French, then English) on the sidewalk at

the corner of First Avenue and East 6th St. in New York City on January 20, 2018. Transcribed by Rachael Guynn Wilson.

By the ... hereby dissolved As described by non-profit The Ocean Cleanup, "The Great Pacific Garbage Patch (GPGP) is the largest of the five offshore plastic accumulation zones in the world's oceans. It is located halfway between Hawaii and California. [...] The GPGP covers an estimated surface area of 1.6 million square kilometers, an area twice the size of Texas or three times the size of France." "The Great Pacific Garbage Patch," *The Ocean Cleanup,* https://theoceancleanup.com/great-pacific-garbage-patch/.

"Will the country ... ever emerge?" Adnan, *Of Cities & Women,* 83.

"blu-a! blu-aa! Ao ... " Muriel Rukeyser, "Foghorn in Horror," *Poetry: A Magazine of Verse* 69, no. 5 (1947): 242.

"Eeeeeenough about ... Plant rights?" Moondog, *H'art Songs* (Kopf, 1978), vinyl record, https://www.discogs.com/master/60563-Moondog-Hart-Songs.

Election Integrity ... enforceable Erasure poem using the text of Executive Order 13820 of January 3, 2018, Termination of Presidential Advisory Commission on Election Integrity, 2024, by Lisa Merschel. Executive Order 13820 disbanded the Presidential Advisory Commission on Election Integrity that Donald Trump had established on May 11, 2017 to review claims of voter fraud in the 2016 Presidential election, including Trump's own false claims that millions of illegal immigrants had voted, causing him to lose the popular vote. No substantive evidence of voter fraud or interference was found. See Michael Tackett and Michael Wines, "Trump Disbands Commission on Voter Fraud," *The New York Times,* January 4, 2018, https://www.nytimes.com/2018/01/03/us/politics/trump-voter-fraud-commission.html.

NOTES TO PAGES 99–108

Lately it ... of #MeToo   These lines refer to several events that occurred in 2018 and 2019. The federal government shut down from midnight on December 22, 2018 until January 25, 2019 (thirty-five days) due to failure to agree on an appropriations bill to fund the government for the 2019 fiscal year. Key to this failure was conflict over Trump's demand for federal funds for a US–Mexico border wall (see note above referencing Trump's 2017 Executive Order 13767 calling for construction of this wall). On January 25, 2019, Trump's longtime associate Roger Stone was indicted as part of special counsel Robert Mueller's investigation into Russian interference in the 2016 US presidential election. Stone was later convicted. Christine Blasey Ford testified before the Senate Judiciary Committee on September 27, 2018, accusing Trump's Supreme Court nominee Brett Kavanaugh of sexually assaulting her. Kavanaugh was confirmed to the Supreme Court on October 6, 2018. The 2018 "migrant caravan," which included persons from Honduras, Guatemala, Nicaragua, and El Salvador, set out toward the United States' southern border from San Pedro Sula, Honduras on October 13, 2018. The caravan became a point of focus for Trump and Republicans leading up the midterm elections of 2018. The #MeToo movement gained momentum in the fall of 2017 after numerous sexual abuse allegations were made against Hollywood film producer Harvey Weinstein. 2018 saw an outpouring of allegations concerning other prominent figures.

Fig. 16   Photo of Santa Rosa neighborhood after the 2018 Tubbs Fire. Photo by California Highway Patrol Golden Gate Division via the Associated Press.

The 14 ... call B.S.   On February 14, 2018, a nineteen-year-old gunman opened fire on students and staff at Marjory Stoneman Douglas High School in Parkland, Florida, killing seventeen people and injuring seventeen more. The shooting set off a new movement against gun violence led by student survivors including X González (formerly Emma González). In a much publicized speech on February 17, 2018, González criticized the government for its failure to enact gun control measures with the refrain "We call B.S." The movement also organized the March for Our Lives rally in Washington, DC on March 24, 2018. Conspiracy theorists claimed that the Parkland students were "crisis actors" paid to advance a political agenda.

Figs. 17–20   From Sacha Archer's *Concrete Poems* [*Repurposed Executive Order*], 2018, ink on paper, in which a printout of Donald Trump's first executive order was crumpled, inked, and stamped to produce a series of visual poems.

We also ... in cages   The Trump administration instituted a policy of separating the families of illegal immigrants along the US–Mexico border, between April 2018 to June 2018. Attorney General Jeff Sessions introduced the policy as a "zero-tolerance" approach intended to deter illegal immigration. Thousands of children were separated from their parents and forcibly held in federal detention centers. Investigations have also revealed that the policy was functionally in effect at the border both before and after the officially authorized period of enactment. During Biden's term as president, more than 25,000 migrant minors were held in federal detention centers at the border annually. See Anna Flagg and Julia Preston, "'No Place for a Child': 1 in 3 Migrants Held in Border Patrol Facilities Is a Minor," *Politico,* June 16, 2022, https://www.politico.com/news/ magazine/2022/06/16 /border-patrol-migrant-children-detention-00039291. Reports as of 2024 noted that many families had still not been reunited.

That the ... massage therapists   See note above (*Lately it ... of #MeToo*) with reference to the "migrant caravan" of 2018.

That Donald ... they want.   On June 12, 2018, at a summit in Singapore Trump became the first US president to meet and shake hands with the leader of North Korea. Trump had previously boasted on Twitter about the size of his "nuclear button" relative to Kim Jong-Un's.

NOTES TO PAGES 108–11

All of ... American "intervention"   The United States government has intervened in the Syrian civil war since 2014 and has continued to support Syrian rebels and Kurdish forces fighting against the Islamic State and president Bashar al-Assad. Under the Trump administration, the US carried out rounds of direct military actions, including missile strikes on Syrian forces in 2017 and 2018. However, Trump abruptly ordered the withdrawal of US troops on December 19, 2018, sparking concerns about the creation of a power vacuum.

Anti-cyber-bullying initiatives ... her husband   As part of her "Be Best" campaign, first lady Melania Trump spoke publicly about the dangers of cyberbullying on August 20, 2018, the same day that her husband took to Twitter to deride the Justice Department and the former CIA director, whom Trump called a "political hack." The first lady did not explicitly denounce the president's behavior on Twitter at this time.

California is NOT burning   The Camp fire, the deadliest wildfire in United States history in one hundred years, began on November 8, 2018 and burned until November 25. Eighty-five people were killed and total damages are estimated at over sixteen billion dollars.

The Iran ... hereby official   On May 8, 2018, the Trump administration announced the United States' withdrawal from the Iran nuclear deal.

There shall ... orange shit-stain-in-chief   See note above (*We also ... in cages*) on the Trump Administration's "zero-tolerance" policy.

"Caw caw ... in [Pittsburgh]"   Allen Ginsberg, *Kaddish and Other Poems: 1958–1960* (City Lights Books, 1961), 36. On October 27, 2018, a gunman killed eleven people and wounded six at the Tree of Life synagogue in Pittsburgh, in the deadliest attack

205

on a Jewish community in United States history. The kaddish is the traditional Jewish prayer of mourning.

Good things ... in Queens   On February 14, 2019, in response to pushback from progressive activists, union leaders, lawmakers, and community members, Amazon called off plans to locate its new headquarters in Long Island City, Queens.

Gray wolves ... species list   Due to population recovery, the US Fish and Wildlife Service announced in March of 2019 that it intended to take gray wolves off the endangered species list.

Roma   A 2018 film by Alfonso Cuarón that depicts the life of a live-in indigenous housekeeper, played by actor Yalitza Aparicio who is of Mixtec and Triqui origin, in Mexico City.

The Squad   Initially a group of four progressive women elected to the House of Representatives in the 2018 midterms: Alexandria Ocasio-Cortez, Ilhan Omar, Ayanna Pressley, and Rashida Tlaib.

Fig. 21   Screenshot from Molly Crabapple's "A Message from the Future with Alexandria Ocasio-Cortez," *The Intercept,* April 17, 2019, video, 7:35, https://theintercept.com/2019/04/17/green-new-deal-short-film-alexandria-ocasio-cortez/.

Attribution studies   A relatively new field of scientific study that measures the impact climate change has on extreme weather events and other events.

Critical Race Theory   Critical race theory is an academic field concerned with the ways ideas about race and ethnicity are embedded in culture and social and political institutions. Previously unknown to the majority of Americans, the term became highly politicized in the lead up to the 2021 midterm elections as a result of conservative backlash.

AMENDMENT 2 ... *be binged*   These lines consist of a homophonic translation of the Second Amendment to the United States Constitution: "A well regulated Militia, being necessary to the security of a free State, the right of the people to keep and bear Arms, shall not be infringed."

Fig. 22   Jenny Holzer, *Truism: Words Tend to Be Inadequate*, 2019, vinyl banner, dimensions unknown. Site-specific banner made for *Franklin Furnace: Performance Is Public* exhibition held at the Central Library branch of Brooklyn Public Libraries, July 15, 2019 to October 15, 2019.

Fig. 23   Photo of climate march in New York City on September 20, 2019, by Amy Howden-Chapman.

The Mueller ... is Halloween   Beginning on May 17, 2017, the Robert Mueller investigation, also called the Russia investigation, probed Trump's involvement in Russian interference in the 2016 presidential election. The result of this inquiry, known as the Mueller report, was published with redactions on April 18, 2019.

The government ... government shutdown   See note above (*Lately it ... of #MeToo*) with reference to the government shutdown of 2018–2019, which lasted thirty-five days and was the longest in the nation's history.

Skolstrejk för klimatet!   Translated from Swedish, this phrase means School Strike for Climate and refers to the Fridays for Future youth climate strike inspired by Greta Thunberg's weekly protests of 2018, during which Thunberg sat outside of Swedish parliament holding a sign with the phrase. In 2019, Thunberg and others organized a series of international climate strikes, including the Global Climate Strikes of March 15 and September 20.

House oversight ... be enforced   The Hatch Act of 1939 prohibits employees in the executive branch of government, other than the president and vice president, from using the powers and privileges of their offices to engage in or support political campaigns. In June of 2019, the US Office of Special Council sent a letter to president Trump recommending that White House counselor Kellyanne Conway be removed from her position for repeatedly violating the Hatch Act.

Free Hong Kong! Between March of 2019 and May of 2020, protests erupted in Hong Kong over the Hong Kong government's introduction of a bill that would effectively authorize case-by-case extradition between Hong Kong and mainland China. Protestors objected to continued erosion of Hong Kong's autonomy, and the corresponding threat to its democracy.

Free Ukraine! Russia invaded Ukraine on February 24, 2022, sparking a major escalation of the ongoing war between the nations that began in 2014.

Free Palestine! Israel has illegally occupied Palestinian territories since 1967. In addition to relocating the US Embassy to Jerusalem (see note above, *Jerusalem is … of Israel*), the Trump administration issued a Presidential Proclamation on Recognizing the Golan Heights as Part of the State of Israel on March 25, 2019. The conflict between Israel and Palestine violently escalated beginning in May of 2021, set off by protests concerning an expected Israeli Supreme Court decision to evict several Palestinian families from the occupied East Jerusalem neighborhood of Sheikh Jarrah.

Fig. 26 See note above regarding the Mueller report (*The Mueller … is Halloween*). Image by Win McNamee/Getty Images.

O, Happy … shall commence, On September 24, 2019, Speaker of the House Nancy Pelosi announced that the House would begin a formal impeachment inquiry over concerns about Trump's involvement in election interference. Democrats alleged that Trump exerted his influence to encourage the president of

Ukraine to initiate a corruption investigation into former Vice President Biden and his son, leading up to the 2020 election. See Nicholas Fandos, "Nancy Pelosi Announces Formal Impeachment Inquiry of Trump," *The New York Times*, September 24, 2019, https://www.nytimes.com/2019/09/24/us/politics/democrats-impeachment-trump.html.

And that ... outstanding subpoena   In September of 2016, state prosecutors in New York subpoenaed Trump's tax returns as part of an investigation into hush money payments to Stormy Daniels, a woman with whom Trump is alleged to have had an extramarital affair. In 2024, Trump was found guilty on all thirty-four counts of conspiring through these payments to influence the 2016 presidential election, making him the first former US president to be convicted as a felon. See William K. Rashbaum and Ben Protess, "8 Years of Trump Tax Returns Are Subpoenaed by Manhattan D.A.," *The New York Times*, September 16, 2019, https://www.nytimes.com/2019/09/16/nyregion/trump-tax-returns-cy-vance.html, and Jonah E. Bromwich and Ben Protess, "Trump Guilty on All Counts in Hush-Money Case," *The New York Times*, May 30, 2024, https://www.nytimes.com/live/2024/05/31/nyregion/trump-news-guilty-verdict.

"Pour conjurer ... exorcisme collectif" / "To banish ... collective exorcism"   Jean-Jacques Lebel, Poster for *Pour conjurer l'esprit de catastrophe* (first version, 1962) in Jean-Jacques Lebel, *Happenings de Jean-Jacques Lebel ou L'insoumission radicale*, ed. Michaël Androula (Hazan, 2009), 48. Lebel's manifesto was published on a poster advertising a happening at Galerie Raymond Cordier in 1962. Translator of passage into English unknown.

We resolve ... a future"   George Robinson, qtd. in Muriel Rukeyser, "From The Book of the Dead: Praise of the Committee," in *The Collected Poems of Muriel Rukeyser*, eds. Janet Kaufman, Anne Herzog, and Jan Levi (University of Pittsburgh Press, 2006).

Fig. 28 Photo of youth climate protest in New York in early spring 2019, by Amy Howden-Chapman.

Hey, everybody ... got impeached!!! President Trump was impeached for the first time on December 18, 2019 when the Democratically controlled House of Representatives adopted two articles of impeachment against him, asserting abuse of power and obstruction of congress. These charges concerned Trump's efforts to invite foreign interference in the 2020 election to serve his re-election campaign, and his obstruction of the House inquiry into these efforts. On February 5, 2020, the Republican held Senate voted to acquit Trump on both articles of impeachment.

"We seem ... Of moonscape" Susan Coolidge, email to Rachael Guynn Wilson of September 27, 2020. The 2020 California wildfire season saw the "August complex fire" in Northern California, which eventually grew to over one million acres, giving rise to the new classification of "gigafire." Fires reached peak levels in September due to record-breaking heat and strong winds.

COVID-19 came ... a vulture The COVID-19 pandemic began with an outbreak in Wuhan, China in December of 2019. The first American case was reported on January 20, 2020. In mid-March of 2020, Trump issued guidelines urging Americans to avoid gathering in groups of ten or more. Soon thereafter, California issued the country's first statewide stay-at-home order. By the end of the calendar year, the Center for Disease Control and Prevention (CDC) reports that there were 350,831 COVID-related deaths in the United States. That number rose dramatically as the pandemic continued.

As the ... shared empathy Kyoo Lee, email message to Rachael Guynn Wilson of December 4, 2021: "Lately, I happened to have been dwelling on this Chinese expression on existential interdependence, 同病相憐 (to translate each character, it could be something like 'common malady, shared empathy') ... and we see how words are not just words, of course."

Mid-May ... murdering them After the murder of George Floyd on May 25, 2020, numerous demonstrations linked to the Black Lives Matter movement occurred at various locations around New York City. The demonstrations continued well into June, and Mayor Bill de Blasio placed the city under curfew from June 1–7. On May 30, an NYPD officer was recorded on video ramming his vehicle into a crowd of gathered demonstrators. For many NYC residents, these events recalled the killing of Eric Garner by NYC police in 2014, which led to a similar eruption of protests. Throughout the country, local police forces responded to protests with shows of extreme force and, in some cases, appeared to encourage or side with right-wing counter-protestors. In Kenosha, Wisconsin, right-wing extremist Kyle Rittenhouse shot and killed two protestors and injured a third on August 25, 2020, during protests that erupted in response to the police shooting of Jacob Blake. As Leah Watson for the ACLU notes, "[Kenosha] Officers enabled and encouraged predominantly white, right-wing armed civilians and militia groups that night, creating a situation in which tensions escalated and people were killed." Leah Watson, "Kyle Rittenhouse Didn't Act Alone: Law Enforcement Must Be Held Accountable," *ACLU News & Commentary,* November 19, 2021, https://www.aclu.org/news/criminal-law-reform/kyle-rittenhouse-didnt-act-alone-law-enforcement-must-be-held-accountable.

"I come ... Have rights" Zianna Oliphant, qtd. in Sam Levin, "'We Shouldn't Have to Feel like This': Girl, Nine, Gives Tearful Speech in Charlotte," *The Guardian,* September 28, 2016, https://www.theguardian.com/us-news/2016/sep/27/keith-scott-killing-charlotte-little-girl-speech-viral.

George Floyd ... Jacob Blake Black Americans killed or seriously injured in incidents in 2020, each of which set off Black Lives Matter protests. Floyd was murdered by police in Minnesota on May 25. Taylor was killed by police in Louisville on March 13. Arbery was murdered by white vigilantes on February 23. Blake was shot seven times by police, resulting in his being paralyzed below the waist, on August 23.

"I just ... fucking country?"   David Perez, qtd. in Jake Offenhartz, Nick Pinto, and Gwynne Hogan, "NYPD's Ambush of Peaceful Bronx Protesters Was 'Executed Nearly Flawlessly,'" *City Leaders Agree," Gothamist,* June 5, 2020, https://gothamist.com/news/nypds-ambush-of-peaceful-bronx-protesters-was-executed-nearly-flawlessly-city-leaders-agree.

8 minutes, 46 seconds later ... 9 minutes, 29 seconds later...   On May 25, 2020, George Floyd was murdered by Minneapolis police officer Derek Chauvin who asphyxiated Floyd by kneeling on his neck for a prolonged period, while Floyd repeatedly stated, "I can't breathe." Shortly afterwards, Hennepin County prosecutors reported the time that Chauvin kneeled on Floyd's neck to be 8 minutes 46 seconds, a number that "became a rallying cry for months at protests in Minneapolis and across the United States." Eventually, the time was revised to 9 minutes 29 seconds, a number that was used in Chauvin's criminal trial in March 2021. Nicholas Bogel-Burroughs, "Prosecutors Say Derek Chauvin Knelt on George Floyd for 9 Minutes 29 seconds, Longer Than Initially Reported," *The New York Times,* March 30, 2021, https://www.nytimes.com/2021/03/30/us/derek-chauvin-george-floyd-kneel-9-minutes-29-seconds.html.

"I believe ... you saw"   Bill de Blasio, qtd. in Offenhartz, Pinto, and Hogan, "NYPD's Ambush of Peaceful Bronx Protesters Was 'Executed Nearly Flawlessly,' City Leaders Agree."

"Last night ... much restraint"   Bill de Blasio, qtd. in "Transcript: Mayor de Blasio Holds Media Availability," *The Official Website of the City of New York,* June 4, 2020, http://www.nyc.gov/office-of-the-mayor/news/406-20/transcript-mayor-de-blasio-holds-media-availability.

"I have ... will be" Bill de Blasio, qtd. in "Floyd Family Transcript: 6/4/20, All In with Chris Hayes," *MSNBC.com*, June 5, 2020, https://www.msnbc.com/transcripts/all-in/2020-06-04-msna1364981.

"The NYPD ... as always" Bill de Blasio, qtd. in Adam K. Raymond Hartmann Margaret, "De Blasio: I Have Not Seen Videos of NYPD Attacking Protesters," *Intelligencer*, June 4, 2020, https://nymag.com/intelligencer/2020/06/mayor-de-blasio-praises-nypd-restraint.html.

Amy Coney ... court bench Trump's nominee Amy Coney Barrett was confirmed to the Supreme Court on October 26, 2020, filling a vacancy created by the death of Justice Ruth Bader Ginsberg on September 18, 2020 — just a week before the presidential election. Such a compressed timeline would be notable in any case, but it stood out particularly against the backdrop of the 2016 stonewalling of President Barack Obama's supreme court nominee Merrick Garland. Garland was to fill the seat vacated by Justice Anthony Scalia, who died on February 13, 2016. Senate Republicans refused to confirm the nomination, stalling until the election could take place in November. Trump's nominee, Neil Gorsuch, was instead confirmed in April 2017. In his single term in office, Trump appointed three Supreme Court justices — the third being Brett Kavanaugh, who filled the seat of Justice Anthony Kennedy, who retired in July 2018.

"Boo! Boo! ... Boo! Boo!" Rob Reiner, dir., *The Princess Bride* (Twentieth Century Fox, 1987), based on a screenplay by William Goldman.

Fig. 29 Screenshot from NBC News, "Fly Lands on Pence's Head, Temporarily Steals Show of 2020 VP Debate | NBC News," *YouTube,* October 8, 2020, https://www.youtube.com/watch?v=wb7yPlCDwRk.

What's that ... is over   During the vice-presidential debate between Mike Pence and Kamala Harris on October 7, 2020, a fly landed on Pence's head and remained there for several moments.

Figs. 30–32   Screenshots from Vice Presidential debate October 7, 2020, with closed captioning.

Saturday, November ... 12 noon   Joe Biden and Kamala Harris were elected president and vice president of the United States on this date in 2020, removing Trump and Pence from office.

The Heavens ... organizers, voters   Stacey Abrams, politician and voting rights activist, was widely credited for helping Joe Biden narrowly win Georgia in the 2020 presidential election.

Fig. 33   Photograph of the Four Seasons Total Landscaping press conference by John Minchillo/Associated Press. After major news networks called the 2020 presidential election for Joe Biden on November 7, Rudy Giuliani, acting as Donald Trump's lawyer, called a press conference on voter fraud, to be held at an obscure landscaping business in the Holmesburg neighborhood of Philadelphia, Pennsylvania. The televised conference took place in front of the garage door of the landscaping business, which, as several reporters noted, was situated between a sex shop and a crematorium. It was inferred that the unusual location was the result of a booking mix-up, and that the intended location was the Four Seasons Hotel in downtown Philadelphia.

They say ... and Wisconsin   "Stop the Steal" was a slogan and far-right protest movement that became prominent soon after the 2020 presidential election in which Joe Biden beat out incumbent Donald Trump. The movement's adherents falsely claim that Biden's win was the result of widespread voter fraud. During a call on January 2, 2020, Trump asked Georgia Secretary of State Brad Raffensperger, a Republican, to help him "find 11,780 votes" to overturn the state's election results, which had favored Biden. Trump and his supporters were also involved in efforts to pressure officials in Michigan, Pennsylvania, Arizona, Texas, Nevada, and Wisconsin to overturn their state election results.

"Did you ... a thing"   Rudy Guiliani, qtd. in Martin Pengelly, "Sweaty Rudy Giuliani Suffers Hair Malfunction in Latest Bizarre Press Conference," *The Guardian,* November 19, 2020, https://www.theguardian.com/us-news/2020/nov/19/rudy-giuliani-dye-my-cousin-vinny-press-conference.

December 8th ... election results   On December 8, 2020, the Supreme Court denied Republican Representative Mike Kelly's lawsuit alleging the unconstitutionality of universal mail-in voting in Pennsylvania and arguing that all mail ballots should be thrown out. On December 11, 2020, the Court declined to hear another case brought by Texas State Attorney General Ken Paxton alleging that Georgia, Michigan, Pennsylvania, and Wisconsin violated the Constitution by changing election procedures concerning mail voting. Voting by mail was especially significant in the 2020 election because of concerns about the impact the COVID-19 pandemic would have on in-person voter turnout.

Even William ... December 23   Trump's Attorney General William Barr issued his resignation on December 23, 2020. Despite serving the Trump administration and its allies, Barr publicly disputed the White House's claims of fraud in the 2020 election.

"I'm working ... fucking break"   Melania Trump, qtd. in Michael D. Shear, "A Recording of Melania Trump Captures Her Complaining in Vulgar Terms about Christmas Decorations and Mocking Detained Migrant Children," *The New York Times,* October 2, 2020, https://www.nytimes.com/2020/10/02/us/elections/a-recording-of-melania-trump-captures-her-complaining-in-vulgar-terms-about-christmas-decorations-and-mocking-detained-migrant-c.html.

Oh, Melania ... do u?" First Lady Melania Trump wore a jacket displaying the phrase "I REALLY DON'T CARE DO U" on June 21, 2018 on a visit to a US–Mexico border facility in Texas housing migrant children who had been separated from their parents under the Trump-era family separation policy. See note above (*We also ... in cages*) referencing the "zero-tolerance" immigration policy. On October 1, 2020, the First Lady was recorded complaining on a personal phone call about criticism of her focus on White House Christmas decorations in light of the ongoing issue of family separation. See above (*"I'm working ... fucking break"*).

Fig. 34 Photo of Melania Trump by Mandel Ngan.

January 6th ... more states 147 Republican members of Congress voted against certifying the election results on the evening of January 6, 2021, not long after the storming of the Capitol building by "Stop the Steal" protestors.

Let's impeach ... Trump twice Trump was impeached a second time on January 13, 2021, when the Democrat-controlled House of Representatives adopted an article of impeachment charging him with incitement of insurrection for his involvement in the January 6 storming of the Capitol. He was again acquitted by the Republican-controlled Senate on February 13, 2021. See note above (*Hey, everybody ... got impeached!!!*) concerning Trump's first impeachment on December 18, 2019.

Players: Senator ... Rush Limbaugh McConnell, Schumer, Greene, Pelosi, Graham, Sanders, and Cruz were members of Congress at the time of Trump's second impeachment. Giuliani publicly bolstered the Trump campaign's allegations of voter fraud (see note above, *"Did you ... a thing,"* referencing the Giuliani press conference). Donald Trump's Tax Returns were subpoenaed in 2016 in the hush-money trial concerning payments to Stormy Daniels (see above note on *"And that ... outstanding subpoena"*). "Horned Rioter" (a.k.a. QAnon Shaman), and "Podium Guy" participated in the January 6 storming of the Capitol, as did the Confederate Flag. Rush Limbaugh, who died on February 17, 2021, was a conservative political commentator awarded the Presidential Medal of Freedom by Trump. Bernie Sanders's Vermont Mittens were prominently featured in a viral photograph of Senator Sanders, runner up for Democratic presidential nominee in 2020, taken at the Biden inauguration on January 20, 2021.

Nancy Pelosi ... commemorative pens   Nancy Pelosi came under fire in January 2020 for using dozens of pens to sign the impeachment articles against Donald Trump and then distributing them to fellow House prosecutors and committee chairmen. Laurie Kellman, "Nancy Pelosi Hands Out Impeachment Pens, a Signing Tradition," *The Associated Press News,* January 16, 2020, https://apnews.com/article/e27aadf061644ba85bf889f2db9d1079.

Nancy Pelosi ... my noggin'!   Cleveland Meredith, Jr. participated in the US Capitol Riots on January 6, 2021 "with a pistol, a rifle and 2,500 rounds of ammunition in his truck." He drove from Colorado to Washington, DC for the Trump rally and insurrection. Upon arriving in DC, Meredith sent a text message to a relative that read "Thinking about heading over to Pelosi CUNT's speech and putting a bullet in her noggin on Live TV" and to which was appended a purple devil emoji. Spencer S. Hsu, "Man Who Drove from Colo. to D.C. on Jan. 6 Pleads Guilty to Threatening to Shoot Pelosi in Head on Live TV," *The Washington Post,* September 10, 2021, https://www.washingtonpost.com/local/legal-issues/pelosi-threat-guilty-plea/2021/09/10/e43066ae-1262-11ec-bc8a-8d9a5b534194_story.html. The word "CUNT's" was redacted from this article but can be found in other reporting on the story.

Ghost of Rush Limbaugh ... broadcast excellence!   The entirety of this speech was transcribed from Rush Limbaugh, "The Rush Limbaugh Show," January 7, 2021.

Senator Ted ... from Cancún In 2021, a major winter storm in the state of Texas caused power outages for 4.5 million homes and businesses between February 10 and 27. 246 people died as a result of the storm, though some estimates count upwards of 700 indirect deaths. Amid the crisis, on February 17, Texas senator Ted Cruz left with his family to Cancún, Mexico for a vacation. Cruz was photographed boarding the plane, and was soon after the subject of public ridicule. He returned to Texas on the 19th. See Shane Goldmacher and Nicholas Fandos, "Ted Cruz's Cancún Trip: Family Texts Detail His Political Blunder," *The New York Times,* February 18, 2021, https://www.nytimes.com/2021/02/18/us/politics/ted-cruz-storm-cancun.html; and *Wikipedia,* s.v. "2021 Texas Power Crisis," https://en.wikipedia.org/w/index.php?title=2021_Texas_power_crisis&oldid=1238682641.

Fig. 35 Brendan Smialowski, working for Agence France-Presse, snapped this photograph of Vermont Senator Bernie Sanders in attendance at Joe Biden's inauguration ceremony on January 21, 2021. The year prior, Sanders ran against Biden to become the Democratic Party's presidential nominee but failed to secure the nomination for the second election cycle in a row. In the photograph, he appears seated in a folding chair with crossed legs and arms folded in his lap. He's dressed in a blue surgical mask, a heavy olive-gray winter coat, and oversized winter mittens (later discovered to be knitted by Jen Ellis, a second-grade schoolteacher in Vermont). Sanders's highly pragmatic attire and perceived ambivalence became the focus of media attention. His dress and demeanor were described as "grumpy chic," "dadcore," and "Vermont grandpa." Smialowski's image in particular became a viral internet meme, as Sanders-in-mittens was inserted into other contexts, and as captions such as, "You coulda had a bad bitch" and "This could have been an email" were appended to the image.

"we do it ... be ashamed" Di Prima, *Revolutionary Letters,* 4.

NOTES TO PAGES 163–72

For "a ... the fire ... " Wilhelm Weitling, qtd. in James Joll, *The Anarchists* (The Anarchist Library, 1979), https:// theanarchistlibrary.org/library/james-joll-the-anarchists.

"Hang in there!" cat ASCII-art style image of a cat dangling mid-air, composed of the phrase "Hang in there!"; after the popular genre of affirmational posters and greeting cards featuring kittens hanging onto tree branches, ropes, and other supports, captioned by the encouraging message: "Hang in there!" Image by the Organism for Poetic Research.

Fig. 36 Photo of Columbia University protest flag by Laura Brown-Lavoie.

We declare ... genocide These and following orders respond to events relating to the Israeli offensive on Gaza and the West Bank that began on October 7, 2023, after Hamas and other Palestinian armed groups breached the Gaza strip's border fence, attacking adjacent areas and killing an estimated 1,139 Israelis and foreign nationals, in addition to taking hundreds as hostages. Israel, led by prime minister Benjamin Netanyahu, retaliated with a full-scale military assault on Gaza, including total blockades on the Gaza strip, as well as increased military control, raids, and airstrikes in the West Bank, all of which continues to intensify as of September 2024. At this time, the United Nations office for the Coordination of Humanitarian Affairs reports more than 41,000 Palestinians killed and approximately 100,000 injured by Israeli attacks. Child fatalities are estimated anywhere between 8,000 and 17,000. The UN reports that 90% of Gaza's 2.1 million population has been displaced, often multiple times. The Israeli blockade on Gaza threatens famine and the outbreak of infectious disease in the region. In January 2024, the United Nation's International Court of Justice (ICJ) determined that Israel's actions against Gaza were "potentially genocidal." "Gaza: ICJ Ruling Offers Hope for Protection of Civilians Enduring Apocalyptic Conditions, Say UN Experts," *United Nations Human Rights Office of the High Commissioner,* January 31, 2024, https://www.ohchr.org/en/press-releases/2024/01/gaza-icj-ruling-offers-hope-protection-civilians-enduring-apocalyptic.

In the US, mass demonstrations for Palestinian solidarity and a ceasefire began in October 2023, with the largest pro-Palestine protest in US history occurring in Washington, DC on November 4, 2023. Pro-Palestine student protests and university encampments started to gain traction in the spring of 2024 and were widespread, both in the US and abroad, by April 2024. In May and June 2024, university administrators began collaborating with local police forces to disrupt, repress, and dismantle student organizing. Students have since been subject to continued harassment, disciplinary action, and legal actions brought against them by their universities.

We say ... for Anyone   The phrase "never again" is commonly employed to invoke a responsibility to prevent and combat genocide. It is particularly associated with Jewish ethics and calls to avert the recurrence an event comparable to the Holocaust. However, it has also been adopted by various groups and causes to signal to a moral responsibility to safeguard all peoples from genocide and fascism. During the Israeli assault on Gaza and the West Bank begun in 2023, the phrase has been used both by supporters of Israeli military actions and by progressives who denounced Israel's killing of tens of thousands of Palestinian civilians in Gaza.

"We've seen ... so high"   Queen Rania of Jordan qtd. in Sana Noor Haq and Claire Calzonetti, "Queen Rania of Jordan Accuses West of 'Glaring Double Standard' as the Death Toll Rises in Besieged Gaza," *CNN*, October 25, 2023, https://www.cnn.com/2023/10/24/middleeast/queen-rania-jordan-amanpour-interview-intl/index.html.

We recognize ... to boycott   The Boycott, Divestment, and Sanctions (BDS) movement calls for international pressure to be put on Israel to end its occupation of Palestine and treatment of Palestinians. On May 17, 2023, a group of Republican Senators introduced the Combatting BDS Act of 2023, which would permit states and local governments to divest from entities engaging in the boycotting, divestment, and sanctioning of Israel. As of 2024, 38 states in the US have passed anti-BDS laws, and the right to boycott has become a topic of much contention in the arts, in publishing, on college campuses, and beyond.

"If you ... one else" Masked Rutgers student in Josh Singer, "Student at Rutgers Speaks Truth to Power Candidly," *YouTube*, May 3, 2024, https://www.youtube.com/watch?v=6gltiNkshhQ.

The United ... United Nations The United States has repeatedly used its veto power to block the passage of United Nations Security Council resolutions condemning Israel. In 2024, the US vetoed several UN resolutions calling for a ceasefire in the war in Gaza. On April 18, 2024, the US also vetoed a UN resolution that would have recognized a Palestinian state and facilitated United Nations membership for Palestine.

"Jean Genet ... the window"' Mahmoud Darwish, qtd. in Helit Yeshurun, "'Exile Is So Strong Within Me, I May Bring It to the Land': A Landmark 1996 Interview with Mahmoud Darwish," *Journal of Palestine Studies* 42, no. 1 (2012): 46–70. (With thanks to Tess Brown-Lavoie for sharing this passage.)

We, the Undersigned Contributors to the volume appear in alphabetical order by last name. Contributors added text and/or images to the manuscript at many different stages of its writing—from its inception in February 2017 to its closure in September 2024. Some contributors have added to the project through the years, but most contributed at a single point in time. None of the "undersigned" have read or "signed off" on the final version of the manuscript, and it's probable that some, if not all, would detract from some parts or aspect of it. We do not intend for the "We, the Undersigned" to represent consensus around the manuscript or any of its poetic or critical statements. The editors alone take responsibility, but not credit, for the ultimate shape of this book. We remain indebted to the collective poetic risk-taking of its contributors.

Excerpts from   The names of writers and artists whose ideas, words, and works we have borrowed and quoted in the book appear in sequence with their order in the main text.

POSTSCRIPT   Though appearing after the "We, the Undersigned" section, the resources in the Postscript were also collaboratively compiled.

Afterword

A Conversation with the Editors
October 2024

Andrew Gorin: It's strange to come to the end of this project at a time that reminds me of its beginning. When we created the *Executive Orders* Google Doc, not long after Trump's election in 2016, everyone we knew was in shock. Since then we've lived through several similar choral outpourings of grief and rage, including those occasioned by the Black Lives Matter protests, the global climate strike, the school shooting in Parkland, the COVID-19 pandemic, the overturning of *Roe v. Wade* and, most recently, Israel's US-supported genocidal campaign in Gaza. In the midst of these compounded crises, we're now heading into the election of 2024 and it feels like history is again repeating itself.

Rachael Guynn Wilson: We were shocked but also galvanized by Trump's election. It wasn't as if we didn't understand the failures of the Obama era and his administration: the expansion of drone warfare, the scandal of NSA surveillance, the holding pattern for mass incarceration, the government bailouts of Wall Street, to name a few. And yet, despite everything, Obama was a powerfully charismatic president, and his administration's tenure seemed to stand for the very idea of incrementalist progressivism, as limited as those horizons may be. Bernie Sanders's performance in the Democratic primaries was another sign that we could move leftward as a nation slowly but surely. But Bernie and his supporters were thwarted by the DNC, then Trump won the 2016 election, and whatever minor optimism we'd had dissolved, or rather imploded.

AG: Right.

RGW: There were some desperate days in that post-election moment. I recall attending a Justice Democrats meetup with a turnout that completely surprised and overwhelmed the organizers, who knew not what to do with this overflowing political energy, and wound up squandering it. People began organizing themselves in ad hoc fashion, creating local action groups. We scrambled to do what we could to create friction within Trump's government, and within the political establishment more broadly. Often, that meant simply calling and writing our representatives, creating boycott lists for companies supporting Trump and his brand, or working at the local level to get leftists and progressives into office.

AG: We also started the "Executive Orders" project, which I think we later came to understand as an exploration of the limits of our political agency as much as a collective expression of our will.

RGW: We did. We were both in grad school at the time and we'd formed a working group that met in an empty classroom at 244 Greene Street. Most of us were poets, all were writers. At some point, someone raised the idea that we should try connecting our creative work to the pragmatic tasks at hand. And so "Executive Orders" emerged as "a project wherein we could respond to the sudden and seemingly relentless barrage of Trump's dystopian executive orders with a series of our own," as we put it in the headnote to the collaborative working document. The impulse to merge our political activities with our poetics sustained the project for a while. But the momentum proved not to be linear or constant. There were periods of dormancy. Until some event would transpire, and another politically focalized moment would emerge, and then we'd be back at it.

AG: The tidal nature of participation in the writing has mirrored the ebb and flow of people's political engagement more generally. And I say this with an eye toward the fact that, for many US residents, political participation seems to mean little more than making and reacting to statements on social media, which is to say that it's not entirely unlike contributing an "executive order" to a collaborative Google Doc. One of the most interesting things about the project has been the way it's served as a barometer of this sort of political energy, in addition to being a record of inciting events that tend to fade too quickly into the background when they are dropped from the news cycle. In other words, it's been a means of attuning to the very tenuous and intermittent sense of political power assumed by people around us.

RGW: I've also been thinking about how Trump's election to the office of POTUS served as impetus for the project, as it did for activist organizing, but then *Executive Orders* quickly branched into wider, and also weirder, territory.

In the US, there's an establishment narrative of Trump-as-crisis, as dangerous anomaly and disruptor of a system whose givenness, naturalness, and soundness itself goes largely unquestioned. In *Executive Orders,* we were interested in understanding Trump as symptomatic of larger underlying problems. Trump (or Trump™) is a recurring character who symbolizes some of the deepest dysfunctions of our political system as well as a cultural low point for the United States, but it's really those underlying conditions to which *Executive Orders* addresses itself.

Another way of saying this: While it was inevitable that Trump drew (and continues to draw) our attention, not only in this project but also in our daily lives, to make this person(-ality) out to be the issue jeopardizing the sociopolitical future of the United States is to play into a vastly oversimplified view of American politics. It's also a romanticized view, in which Democrats and Republicans can turn up on the same side of the aisle, not because they similarly belong to and are beholden to the wealthiest segment of the population — as it really is — but because a chaotic, destructive outsider force has united them on the side of the good (the side of "democracy"). Cue the *Good Morning America* and CBS News specials on George W. Bush and Michelle Obama's friendship circa 2018. Let historical memory melt away in the exchange of candy at John McCain's funeral. In fact, these are exactly the kind of details *Executive Orders* captures. It sort of approaches its subject from below.

AG: I think that the way Trump has served, in and beyond *Executive Orders,* as a political lightning rod, albeit one indicative of a much larger storm bearing down on the United States, as you say, is actually key to what I take to be one of the text's most important satirical functions. While *Executive Orders* is an experiment in utopian dream-wishing, it's also an effort to deflate Trump's executive authority — and thus his centrality — by rendering executive pronouncements like his both highly provisional and absurd. This means that *Executive Orders* is conscious and critical of its own aggrandizing and authoritative rhetoric. And it is critical of this rhetoric in a way that seeks to imaginatively diminish Trump's authority while simultaneously recognizing that performative denunciations of what are merely prominent symptoms of systemic problems, even where these denunciations come from political sectors that we deem laudable, are in themselves insufficient. This is one reason why previous published versions of *Executive Orders* included a postscript listing actions one might take and organizations one might contribute to or get involved with to support progressive politics and social justice. So, to get back to your point: I agree that this writing could seem to put Trump at the center in a manner that might be deemed naive. But in important respects, this critically mirrors how voices on the Left (and on the internet) often focus on attention-grabbing events and public figures in a way that might produce an energized base but also sometimes takes the conversation in the direction of spectacle rather than substance.

RGW: It seems to me that none of us knows how revolutionary change occurs. How, even, do we create dissensus, or open up spaces of counter-hegemonic praxis? Consider, for example, the irony of the day: that so much leftist organizing is both facilitated by and beholden to some of the worst privately owned corporate platforms out there (namely, Meta and X, at the moment). What happens to oppositional speech as it surfaces within and binds itself to such corporate media technologies? As Audre Lorde once wrote, when we use the "master's tools" in our resistance efforts, "It means that only the most narrow perimeters of change are possible and allowable."[1] But let me just say again that none of us really know how revolutionary change occurs. There are, however, credible reasons to believe that language might be a key agent.

Elsewhere, we've discussed J.L. Austin's theory of performative language in relation to this project. Performatives, per Austin, are utterances that aspire to make things happen in the world as a direct result of the utterance. He also calls them "speech acts" and gives the example of someone marrying a couple by saying, "I now pronounce you man and wife," or making a bet by saying, "I bet you 'X.'"[2] This is a dramatized version of the way that speech can effect change, and one that's relevant to our project, which focuses on the speech act of a sovereign or "executive" leader giving an order ("I hereby decree…"). Austin's theory of speech acts calls attention to this novel category of language, which feels a bit like a sorcerer's language: you say the magic words and the enchantment, or "spell," is cast. I suppose part of the broad appeal of Austin's theory derives from

---

1   Audre Lorde, *Sister Outsider,* reprint edition (Crossing Press, 2007), 111.
2   See J.L. Austin, *How to Do Things with Words* (Harvard University Press, 1962).

its association with a longer history of connecting language to magic and power. It's a deep-rooted idea that language has special power to affect the material world. We don't need to put stock in magic to understand that this concept may arise from something real — from an experience of the power of rhetoric to shape feelings, sway opinions, and cause people to act in various ways. The speech act, then, presents an amplified expression of the pervasive but otherwise latent capacity of all language to "perform." Rhetoric, in other words, is never merely rhetorical.

Still, I agree with your assessment of a major problem in leftist political organizing: that it's easy for people to get swept up in a reactive mode of political engagement, to be consumed by perpetual crisis, and that this fight-or-flight mode of engagement inhibits the longer-game movement building that we desperately need. We *should* put stock in language, though we also need to be thinking about what will make our speech effective, or, as Austin puts it, "felicitous." Not every spell comes off right. You might turn your mother into a horse while trying to turn the king into a toad. One has to be careful about these things.

AG: You have to be careful, but sometimes you also have to risk turning your mother into a horse, i.e., you have to risk being taken for an ineffectual buffoon more interested in the discursive performance of revolutionary politics (online and wherever else) than in pragmatic organizing. On the other hand, performative assertions in media spaces are potentially very pragmatic and effectual. This is especially true in the case of the mobilization of virtual mass publics or "imagined communities," which by definition only exist for our contemplation as an effect of the rhetoric that brings them into being.

One of the original inspirations for *Executive Orders* was Allen Ginsberg's performative declaration of the end of the Vietnam War in his 1966 poem "Wichita Vortex Sutra," the text of which appeared broken into two segments in the first published version of the *Executive Orders* project as follows:

> I lift my voice aloud,
>   make Mantra of American language now,
>   I here declare the end of the War!
>   Ancient days' Illusion! —
>   and pronounce words beginning my own millennium.
> […]
> Let the States tremble,
> let the nation weep,
>   let Congress legislate its own delight,
>   let the President execute [her] own desire —
> this Act done by my own voice,
>   nameless Mystery —
> published to my own senses,
>   blissfully received by my own form
> approved with pleasure by my sensations
>   manifestation of my very thought
>   accomplished in my own imagination
>   all realms within my consciousness fulfilled.³

In the Google Doc, someone pretty quickly changed the pronoun "his" to "her" in the fourth line of the second segment, so that Ginsberg's language is converted into a wishful enactment of the election of a female President. But apart from that gesture to an imagined feminist voting base, these lines are a particularly apt example of the work that the rhetorical invocation of publics can do because they were originally a response to what is probably the most infamous *abuse* of this power in American history: the US government, policy elite, and media's false representation of the American people's opinion on intervention in Vietnam (elsewhere in his poem, Ginsberg writes that "The war is language, / language abused"). Incidentally, it was Bruce Andrews, another poet and a scholar of foreign policy, who first marshaled statistical evidence to claim that the US government's

---

3   Allen Ginsberg qtd. in *Executive Orders, vol. 1* (Organism for Poetic Research, 2017). For Ginsberg's complete poem see "Wichita Vortex Sutra," in *Planet News: 1961–1967* (City Lights, 2001), 119.

portrayal of the American people as pro-war at the time was in fact a lie.[4] Ginsberg's magical declaration of the end of the war, then, responds in kind to the Johnson administration's bad-faith magical thinking on the popularity of American hawkishness. The self-conscious performativity of his lines undermines top-down representations of the American public while also proposing the existence of individuals who might have different attitudes about the war from the one being commonly attributed to them. Insofar as concrete political actions are often justified through reference to the will of such collectives, how we imagine and reimagine collectivities matters. My hope is that *Executive Orders* dramatizes this fact in fruitful ways.

RGW: All of this. We see the way that our supposedly "representative" form of government has exploited the gross power imbalances brought into being by unfettered capitalism in order to dispossess people, on ever-wider scales, of a voice in politics. You might say Ginsberg's poem counters a deep fake with the ecstatic truth!

AG: Absolutely. And the term "deep fake" brings us back to the urgency of such countermoves in a present in which public opinion is more manipulable than ever.

RGW: Yes. And at present, we find ourselves entering a historical loop as Trump and Biden face off as the presumptive nominees of their respective parties for the 2024 election. And yet, both candidates are dramatically unpopular according to most polls, which goes to show, yet again, how dysfunctional our sys-

---

[4] See Bruce Andrews, *Public Constraint and American Policy in Vietnam* (Sage Publications, 1976). Howard Zinn cites Andrews to make the point that "the media, themselves controlled by higher-education, higher-income people who were more aggressive in foreign policy, tended to give the erroneous impression that working-class people were superpatriots for the war." Zinn, *A People's History of the United States: 1492–Present* (Harper Perennial Modern Classics, 2015), 492.

tem has become. The dominant parties and their politicians are insulated from public opinion and lack basic accountability.

Critics like Noam Chomsky have thoroughly dissected the way in which powerful financial interests control the US political system, effectively voiding popular representation and stymying the popular will when and where it arises. It is difficult to imagine how we might address the deeply stacked situation we find ourselves in today and transform our conditions deliberately, rather than through the effects of cataclysm.

What on earth can poets do?

AG: Well, maybe one thing poets and cultural workers more generally can do is help us keep track of something difficult to measure by more quantitative means: the status of the cultural sphere wherein the experience and will of collectives gets represented so that it might translate into action. Sociology's term for this sphere is the public sphere. And when I say it's difficult to measure, I mean that, as the co-production of all those who participate in it, it is constantly changing in space and time. To be sure, the public sphere is undergirded by concrete institutions like newspapers, social media platforms, publishing houses, town hall meetings, and film studios, etc. But it's always greater than the sum of these parts, not least because it is additionally comprised of the ever-evolving soft infrastructure of norms and conventions that each of us must imagine or perform when entering it. It could be defined as the total amalgamation of all possible ways of conceiving of these conventions and norms.

In this respect, the public sphere is probably best understood as the set of rhetorical orientations and modes of comportment that people take up in public discourse, rather than as concrete institutions or discursive spaces. Humanistic culture has played a key role in reflecting on these orientations and modes of comportment, both overtly and implicitly (this is actually the reason why I do research on literature and media), and I think that poetry, which is still often framed as "privacy made public," has had an especially important historical relation to the shifting ideals of publicness precisely because it's been so frequently positioned on the threshold where publicness begins.

What, then, can a project like *Executive Orders* do? Well, I think one of the things it can do — one of the things it does do — is provide a sort of snapshot of the power gap between public opinion and government that we've been discussing. There's a funny way that this makes the project both ineffectual and about ineffectuality in a potentially effectual manner. But it can also explore this ineffectuality to point to alternative spaces for deliberation and action.

RGW: I've been reading Ammiel Alcalay and Simone White recently — a manuscript by Ammiel called CONTROLLED DEMOLITION and one by Simone called *Warring* — and both of these poets have got me thinking in new ways about the questions we keep circling here, in this conversation and in this project.

In *Warring*, Simone White uses poetics as a space in which to produce dissensus, or, at least, to amplify what is a kind of managed dissensus elsewhere in our culture. Her work effectively desegregates the discourses of philosophy in/of the Black radical tradition and Black studies and that of trap music. Meeting in her listening, her language, and her feeling, they struggle to coexist, to find a container or logic that mutually holds them. Their continued encounter, we feel, might even force a new logos. Trap music, White contends, "requires consideration of the possibility that resistance belongs to an ideological logic of sorting that isn't oppositional in the way we used to think it was."[5]

There might be a similar discovery in CONTROLLED DEMOLITION, in which Ammiel Alcalay magpies shards of a recent history of American empire to render its likeness — that of a machine for amassing power and control, politically, militarily, economically, and culturally — with terrible clarity. He reveals patterns of ideological misdirection and disinformation so deep

---

5 Simone White, *Warring* (Duke University Press, forthcoming).

I begin to question the concept of a "bottom," and he posits that the state's ultimate aim is to have us "begin any inquiry at a point that precludes and eliminates the most important questions."[6]

As in Ammiel's work, we must keep inventing ways to ask the other questions, the "wrong" questions, to refuse that which is given (from above), and to affirm that which we know most intimately as another possible, and perhaps realer, reality. As in Simone's work, we have to keep holding impossible and incommensurate realities together until we force another logos. That each and any of us can perform this work, and is responsible for doing so, is the bid of Executive Orders. It's a terrifying thought, but we must all become poets.

AG: I think that terrifying urge toward poetic becoming is a good place for this conversation to end.

RGW: "So be it disordered."

---

[6] Ammiel Alcalay, *CONTROLLED DEMOLITION: a work in four books* (Litmus Press, 2025), 531.

Bibliography

"2019 Word of the Year Is '(My) Pronouns,' Word of the Decade Is Singular 'They.'" *American Dialect Society*, January 4, 2020. https://americandialect.org/2019-word-of-the-year-is-my-pronouns-word-of-the-decade-is-singular-they/.

Acker, Kathy. *Blood and Guts in High School*. Grove Press, 1989.

Adnan, Etel. *Of Cities & Women: Letters to Fawwaz*. Post-Apollo Press, 1993.

Alcalay, Ammiel. *CONTROLLED DEMOLITION: a work in four books*. Litmus Press, 2025.

Austin, J.L. *How to Do Things with Words*. Harvard University Press, 1962.

Baraka, Amiri [LeRoi Jones]. *Black Magic: Poetry 1961–1967*. Bobbs-Merrill, 1969.

Baumer, Mark. "A guy who doesn't believe in human induced climate change gave me a dollar." *YouTube*, November 10, 2016. https://www.youtube.com/watch?v=CdV2AlU88UY.

———. "Our Bodies Are Machines Built to Force so Much Compassion, Kindness, and Love into the World Human Life Has No Choice but to Thrive and Flourish." *Barefoot Across America*, November 10, 2016. https://notgoingtomakeit.com/my-body-is-a-machine-built-to-force-so-much-compassion-kindness-and-love-into-the-world-human-a5d492d874e5.

Bogel-Burroughs, Nicholas. "Prosecutors Say Derek Chauvin Knelt on George Floyd for 9 Minutes 29 seconds, Longer Than Initially Reported." *The New York Times,* March 30, 2021. https://www.nytimes.com/2021/03/30/us/derek-chauvin-george-floyd-kneel-9-minutes-29-seconds.html.

Bromwich, Jonah E., and Ben Protess, "Trump Guilty on All Counts in Hush-Money Case." *The New York Times,* May 30, 2024. https://www.nytimes.com /live/2024/05/31/nyregion/trump-news-guilty-verdict.

Brooks, Gwendolyn. "BOYS. BLACK. *a preachment."* In *Beckonings.* Broadside Press, 1975.

Carson, Rachel. *Silent Spring.* Houghton Mifflin, 1962.

Césaire, Aimé. *Discourse on Colonialism.* Translated by Joan Pinkham. Monthly Review Press, 2001.

———. *Notebook of a Return to the Native Land.* Wesleyan University Press, 2001.

Coates, Ta-Nehisi. *Between the World and Me.* Random House, 2015.

Delk, Josh. "Trump Refers to Virgin Islands Governor as Its 'President.'" *The Hill,* October 13, 2017. https://thehill.com / blogs/blog-briefing-room/355377-trump-calls-governor-of-virgin-islands-its-president/.

Derrida, Jacques. "Declarations of Independence." *New Political Science* 7, no. 1 (1986): 7–15. DOI: 10.1080/07393148608429608.

di Prima, Diane. *Revolutionary Letters.* City Lights Books, 1971.

Eisenstein, Sergei. *Selected Works: Vol. I, Writings, 1922–34.* Edited and translated by Richard Taylor. University of Indiana Press, 1988.

El violinista del amor & los pibes que se miraban. *Contra Los Fantasmas: Canciones e Himnos de Revoluciones Que No Fueron.* Buenos Aires, 2013. Digital album. https://elviolinista delamorylospibesquemiraban.bandcamp.com/album/contra-los-fantasmas-2013.

Fandos, Nicholas. "Nancy Pelosi Announces Formal Impeachment Inquiry of Trump." *The New York Times,*

September 24, 2019. https:// www.nytimes.com/2019/09/24/us/politics/democrats-impeachment-trump.html.

Flagg, Anna, and Julia Preston. "'No Place for a Child': 1 in 3 Migrants Held in Border Patrol Facilities Is a Minor." *Politico,* June 16, 2022. https://www.politico.com/news/magazine/2022/06/16 /border-patrol-migrant-children-detention-00039291.

Florido, Adrian. "Picture an America with #TacoTrucksOnEveryCorner." *NPR,* September 2, 2016. https://www.npr.org/sections/codeswitch/2016/09/02/492446419/picture-an-america-with-tacotrucksoneverycorner.

Flaubert, Gustave. *Bouvard and Pécuchet.* Translated by T.W. Earp and G.W. Stonier. New Directions, 1954.

"Floyd Family Transcript: 6/4/20, All In with Chris Hayes." *MSNBC.com,* June 5, 2020. https://www.msnbc.com/transcripts/all-in/2020-06-04-msna1364981.

Foster, Hal. "The Artist as Ethnographer." In *The Traffic in Culture: Refiguring Art and Anthropology,* edited by George E. Marcus and Fred R. Myers. University of California Press, 1995.

"Gaza: ICJ Ruling Offers Hope for Protection of Civilians Enduring Apocalyptic Conditions, Say UN Experts." *United Nations Human Rights Office of the High Commissioner,* January 31, 2024. https://www.ohchr.org/en/press-releases/2024/01/gaza-icj-ruling-offers-hope-protection-civilians-enduring-apocalyptic.

Gins, Madeline. *What the President Will Say and Do!* Station Hill Press, 1984.

Ginsberg, Allen. *Kaddish and Other Poems: 1958–1960.* City Lights Books, 1961.

———. "Wichita Vortex Sutra." In *Planet News: 1961–1967.* City Lights, 2001.

Goldmacher, Shane, and Nicholas Fandos. "Ted Cruz's Cancún Trip: Family Texts Detail His Political Blunder." *The New York Times,* February 18, 2021. https://www.nytimes.com/2021/02/18/us/politics/ted-cruz-storm-cancun.html.

Graham, David A. "Donald Trump's Favorite Topic for Black History Month: Himself." *The Atlantic,* February 1, 2017. https://www.theatlantic.com/politics/archive/2017/02/frederick-douglass-trump/515292/.

Haq, Sana Noor, and Claire Calzonetti. "Queen Rania of Jordan Accuses West of 'Glaring Double Standard' as the Death Toll Rises in Besieged Gaza." *CNN,* October 25, 2023. https://www.cnn.com/2023/10/24/middleeast/queen-rania-jordan-amanpour-interview-intl/index.html.

hooks, bell. *Black Looks: Race and Representation.* South End Press, 1992.

Hsu, Spencer S. "Man Who Drove from Colo. to D.C. on Jan. 6 Pleads Guilty to Threatening to Shoot Pelosi in Head on Live TV." *The Washington Post,* September 10, 2021. https://www.washingtonpost.com/local/legal-issues/pelosi-threat-guilty-plea/2021/09/10/e43066ae-1262-11ec-bc8a-8d9a5b534194_story.html.

Joll, James. *The Anarchists.* The Anarchist Library, 1979. https://theanarchistlibrary.org/library/james-joll-the-anarchists.

Kellman, Laurie. "Nancy Pelosi Hands out Impeachment Pens, a Signing Tradition." *The Associated Press News,* January 16, 2020. https://apnews.com/article/e27aadf061644ba85bf889f2db9d1079.

Kilani, Hazar. "'Asthma Alley': Why Minorities Bear Burden of Pollution Inequity Caused by White People." *The Guardian,* April 4, 2019. https://www.theguardian.com/us-news/2019/apr/04/new-york-south-bronx-minorities-pollution-inequity.

Lau, Tim. "Citizens United Explained." *Brennan Center for Justice,* December 12, 2019. https://www.brennancenter.org/our-work/research-reports/citizens-united-explained.

Lebel, Jean-Jacques. *Happenings de Jean-Jacques Lebel ou L'insoumission radicale.* Edited by Michaël Androula. Hazan, 2009.

Levin, Sam. "'We Shouldn't Have to Feel like This': Girl, Nine, Gives Tearful Speech in Charlotte." *The Guardian,* September 28, 2016. https://www.theguardian.com/

us-news/2016/sep/27/keith-scott-killing-charlotte-little-girl-speech-viral.

Lorde, Audre. *Sister Outsider.* Reprint edn. Crossing Press, 2007.

Martinelli, Marissa. "Jon Stewart Turns a Late Show Bit About Trump's Executive Orders Into a Rousing Call to Action." *Slate,* February 1, 2017. https://slate.com /culture/2017/02/jon-stewart-reads-fake-trump-executive-orders-to-stephen-colbert-on-the-late-show-video.html.

Moondog. *H'art Songs.* Kopf, 1978. Vinyl record. https://www.discogs.com/master/60563-Moondog-Hart-Songs.

NBC News. "Fly Lands on Pence's Head, Temporarily Steals Show of 2020 VP Debate | NBC News." *YouTube,* October 8, 2020. https://www.youtube.com/watch?v=wb7yPlCDwRk.

Offenhartz, Jake, Nick Pinto, and Gwynne Hogan. "NYPD's Ambush of Peaceful Bronx Protesters Was 'Executed Nearly Flawlessly,' City Leaders Agree." *Gothamist,* June 5, 2020. https://gothamist.com/news/nypds-ambush-of-peaceful-bronx-protesters-was-executed-nearly-flawlessly-city-leaders-agree.

O'Hara, Frank. *The Collected Poems of Frank O'Hara.* University of California Press, 1995.

Ono, Yoko. *Grapefruit: A Book of Instructions and Drawings by Yoko Ono.* Simon & Schuster, 1964.

Peck, Raoul, dir. *I Am Not Your Negro.* Artémis Productions, 2017.

Pengelly, Martin. "Sweaty Rudy Giuliani Suffers Hair Malfunction in Latest Bizarre Press Conference." *The Guardian,* November 19, 2020. https://www.theguardian.com /us-news/2020/nov/19/rudy-giuliani-dye-my-cousin-vinny-press-conference.

Popovich, Nadja, Livia Albeck-Ripka, and Kendra Pierre-Louis. "The Trump Administration Rolled Back More Than 100 Environmental Rules. Here's the Full List." *The New York Times,* October 16, 2020. https:// www.nytimes.com/interactive/2020/climate/trump-environment-rollbacks-list.html.

Rankine, Claudia, and Beth Loffreda. "On Whiteness and The Racial Imaginary." *Literary Hub,* April 9, 2015. https://lithub.com/on-whiteness-and-the-racial-imaginary/.

Rashbaum, William K., and Ben Protess. "8 Years of Trump Tax Returns Are Subpoenaed by Manhattan D.A." *The New York Times,* September 16, 2019. https://www.nytimes.com/2019/09/16/nyregion/trump-tax-returns-cy-vance.html.

Reiner, Rob, dir. *The Princess Bride.* Twentieth Century Fox, 1987.

Robb, Graham. *Victor Hugo: A Biography.* W.W. Norton & Company, 1997.

Rukeyser, Muriel. "Foghorn in Horror." *Poetry: A Magazine of Verse* 69, no. 5 (1947): 4. https://www.poetryfoundation.org/poetrymagazine/browse?volume=69&issue=5&page=4.

———. "From The Book of the Dead: Praise of the Committee." In *The Collected Poems of Muriel Rukeyser,* edited by Janet Kaufman, Anne Herzog, and Jan Levi. University of Pittsburgh Press, 2006.

Sharp, Willoughby. "An Interview with Joseph Beuys." *Artforum,* December 1, 1969. https://www.artforum.com/features/an-interview-with-joseph-beuys-210674/.

Shear, Michael D. "A Recording of Melania Trump Captures Her Complaining in Vulgar Terms about Christmas Decorations and Mocking Detained Migrant Children." *The New York Times,* October 2, 2020. https://www.nytimes.com/2020/10/02/us/elections/a-recording-of-melania-trump-captures-her-complaining-in-vulgar-terms-about-christmas-decorations-and-mocking-detained-migrant-c.html.

Singer, Josh. "Student at Rutgers Speaks Truth to Power Candidly." *YouTube,* May 3, 2024. https://www.youtube.com/watch?v=6gltiNkshhQ.

Tackett, Michael, and Michael Wines. "Trump Disbands Commission on Voter Fraud." *The New York Times,* January 4, 2018. https://www.nytimes.com/2018/01/03/us/politics/trump-voter-fraud-commission.html.

"The Great Pacific Garbage Patch." *The Ocean Cleanup.* https://theoceancleanup.com/great-pacific-garbage-patch/.

"The Social Cost of Greenhouse Gases (Carbon Dioxide, Methane, Nitrous Oxide)." *Environmental and Energy Law Program,* Harvard Law School. https://eelp.law.harvard.edu/tracker/the-social-cost-of-carbon/.

"Transcript: Mayor de Blasio Holds Media Availability." *The Official Website of the City of New York,* June 4, 2020. http://www.nyc.gov/office-of-the-mayor/news/406-20/transcript-mayor-de-blasio-holds-media-availability.

Trinh T. Minh-Ha. *Woman, Native, Other: Writing Postcoloniality and Feminism.* Indiana University Press, 1989.

Watson, Leah. "Kyle Rittenhouse Didn't Act Alone: Law Enforcement Must Be Held Accountable." *ACLU News & Commentary,* November 19, 2021. https://www.aclu.org/news/criminal-law-reform/kyle-rittenhouse-didnt-act-alone-law-enforcement-must-be-held-accountable.

White, Simone. *Warring.* Duke University Press, forthcoming.

Yeshurun, Helit. "'Exile Is So Strong Within Me, I May Bring It to the Land': A Landmark 1996 Interview with Mahmoud Darwish." *Journal of Palestine Studies* 42, no. 1 (2012): 46–70. DOI: 10.1525/jps.2012.xlii.1.46.

Zinn, Howard. *A People's History of the United States: 1492–Present.* Harper Perennial Modern Classics, 2015.

Acknowledgments

For their crucial role in seeding and stewarding this project, we wish to thank past and present members of The Organism for Poetic Research—Kimberly Adams, Louise Akers, Timothy Anderson, Alliya Dagman, David Hobbs, Caitlin Hurst, MC Hyland, Zane Koss, John Melillo, Anna Moser, Urayoán Noel, Nate Preus, Daniel C. Remein, Lytle Shaw, Ada Smailbegović, Kristen Tapson, and Cameron Williams—and the NYC Action Group Members.

For generously hosting "Executive Orders" events, thanks to the staff at the Brooklyn Public Library, with a special shout out to Nomi Muhammad and Melissa Morrone, as well as to Brooklyn Art Library and Quimby's Bookstore NYC. We're grateful to The Brooklyn Arts Council for their help funding these events. For publishing this project at various stages of its life, thanks to Elæ Moss and Joe Cogen at The Operating System, and to Wendy's Subway + Emily Carr University's Libby Leshgold Gallery for "Publishing the Present: An Archive of Mutual Care and Action." For spreading the word and giving us a platform to present this work, thanks to Ian Dreiblatt and MobyLives, a Melville House blog, the Poetry Foundation's Harriet, Aaron Cohick of AMPLIFY & MULTIPLY: Recent Printed Activist Ephemera, and Art Resources Transfer. Additionally, thanks to the event organizers, fellow panelists, and audience-participants at the Flow Chart Foundation's 2023 Gathering in Hudson, New York, and the 2023 HASTAC: Critical Making & Social Justice conference in Brooklyn, and to panel organizer

Kathleen Naughton, fellow presenters, and audience at the 2024 Modern Language Association (MLA) conference in Philadelphia. For their involvement and support in various ways and at various points along the way, our gratitude to Amy Howden-Chapman and Garth Swanson. Thanks to our poetry/community named above and to those at Belladonna* Collaborative, Bushel Collective, Litmus Press, Poetry Corp, The Poetry Project, and Pratt — including fellow travelers Bahaar Ahsan, Ammiel Alcalay, Miriam Atkin, Jordan Behr, Jonathan Beller, Dan Boscov-Ellen, Tess Brown-Lavoie, Caitlin Cahill, Caroline Crumpacker, Iris Cushing, Mike de Soto, Claire DeVoogd, Marcella Durand, Alexandra Egan, Mel Ehlberg, Fyn Elrick, Levy Erwin, Will Fesperman, Jennifer Firestone, Jessica Flemming, Gabe Flores, Elaine Freedgood, Regan Good, David Gorin, Tracy Grinnell, Anna Gurton-Wachter, HR Hegnauer, Laura Henriksen, Ann Holder, Bethany Ides, Nurhaizatul Jamil, erica kaufman, Sahar Khraibani, Chime Lama, Krystal Languell, Kyoo Lee, Rachel Levitsky, James Loop, Zak Margolis, Emily Martin, Lola Milholland, A. Monti, Anna Moschovakis, Garrett Phelps, Ru Puro, Gary Robbins, Gerónimo Sarmiento Cruz, Stacy Skolnik, Sparrow, Sara Jane Stoner, Zoe Tuck, Morgan Võ, Alisha Wessler, Simone White, Elizabeth Willis, Summer Wrobel, Matvei Yankelevich, and many others who have encouraged and inspired us along the way.

Heaps of gratitude to Matthew Thurber for the inspired cover artwork, and to Mark Nowak, Juliana Spahr, and Rodrigo Toscano for so generously offering their words to accompany this book into the world. Deepest thanks, too, to our publishers, Vincent W.J. van Gerven Oei and Eileen A. Fradenburg Joy, at the radical punctum books.

We acknowledge that Executive Orders has been edited, published, and performed on colonized lands — specifically, on the traditional and unceded lands of the Lenape. Work for this project was also carried out in New York City during the height of the COVID-19 pandemic. We wish to thank the frontline and essential workers who helped keep the City afloat during this period. Thanks also to the demonstrators, to the people agitating on the streets then and now, resisting injustice and cynicism with their bodies, spirit, intellect, and voices.

To the memories of poet-heroes recently lost: Joshua Clover, Lyn Hejinian, Pierre Joris, Bernadette Mayer, and Alice Notley.

And to Hart, Talia, and all the kids.

Finally, the editors wish to thank all contributors to *Executive Orders*. Thank you for trusting us with your orders. We *will* see that they take effect.

www.ingramcontent.com/pod-product-compliance
Lightning Source LLC
Chambersburg PA
CBHW071001160426
43193CB00012B/1870